Memories, Miracles & Meaning

Insights of a Holocaust Survivor

FANNY KRASNER LEBOVITS

with Selwyn Isakow and Sid Shapira

www.mascotbooks.com

Memories, Miracles & Meaning

For more information, please contact:
Mascot Books
620 Herndon Parkway, Suite 320
Herndon, VA 20170
info@mascotbooks.com

Library of Congress Control Number: 2018909953

CPSIA Code: PBANG1018A
ISBN-13: 978-1-64307-190-9

Printed in the United States

Dedicated to my parents, Sarah and Herman; sisters, Jenny and Liebele; children, Harold, Shirley, Milton, and Marc; and nine grandchildren, thirteen great-grandchildren, and their future generations.

MAY WE LEARN FROM THE PAST AND NEVER FORGET.

MAY WE LEARN FROM OUR HERITAGE AND CONDUCT OURSELVES ACCORDINGLY.

MAY WE UNDERSTAND THAT HATE IS NEVER GOOD AND LOVE IS NEVER BAD.

The biggest miracle of all is that we, the survivors of the Holocaust, after all that we witnessed and lived through, still believe and have faith in the Almighty God, may His name be blessed. This, my friends, is the miracle of miracles, the greatest miracle ever to have taken place.

—Rabbi Yekutiel Yehuda Halberstam from Romania, whose wife and eleven children and most of his followers were murdered by the Nazis while he was incarcerated in several concentration camps

GRANNY FANNY

You touch so many.
Unique, bold, brave, generous, selfless and kind
Are just a few words that come to mind.
Survival, strength and perseverance are the things I admire,
And at 90 years old, your eyes still reflect that fire.
You are an inspiration to all those you meet.
And to find one as courageous as you would be not an easy feat.
Throughout the ninety years of your life that we celebrate,
You have always held strong morals that truly emanate.
Family and Jewish tradition are the center of our lives.
It is because of you that these strong values will continue to survive.
Your children, grandchildren and great-grandchildren
are your greatest pleasure,
But really the love we have for you, is hard to measure!
You have shared with us your love of life and Israel,
Which we will forever support and promise not to fail.
Everyone here is truly blessed to know you,
We honor and respect you for all that you do.
You have taught us to be strong and never give up,
And now in honor of you, Granny, I ask that we all raise a cup!
May we all live to be as healthy, strong, wise and beautiful as you!

—TOAST DELIVERED AT FANNY'S NINETIETH
BIRTHDAY CELEBRATION IN 2012 BY HER
GRANDDAUGHTER STACY VARON.

Table of Contents

FOREWORD

Spiritual leaders tell us there are no coincidences in life, just the silent hand of a greater being influencing events. This is the story of an amazing woman. Her experiences reflect the nadir of physical and psychological human struggles and the pinnacle of family joy and personal fulfillment that helped mitigate previous pain and sorrow.

But the coincidences that occurred along this difficult road can only be explained as a series of miracles, even to the most ontologically skeptical. Fanny Krasner Lebovits's life story makes one think that each of us has a purpose on this earth. As Shakespeare wrote in Hamlet, "There's a divinity that shapes our ends; rough hew them how we will."

Fanny survived the Liepāja ghetto in Latvia and the horrors of five Nazi concentration camps during World War II. She is one of less than 2 percent of the approximately nine thousand Jews from her town to live through the Holocaust.

Sitting amid those gathered at Congregation Beth El in La Jolla, California, each Yom Kippur, I would listen to Fanny tell her heartbreaking World War II stories. She would end her address by singing a song written in the Warsaw ghetto about despair, belief, and hope. At age ninety-five and less than five feet tall, Fanny always needed to stand on a stool to peer over the lectern. Yet it was clear to all she had the tallest personality of the eight hundred congregants in the room.

As I spent more time with this remarkable woman of valor, I became completely enraptured by her story of triumph and success. Her triumph in overcoming the challenges she faced over and again. Her success in love, family, caring for others, business, and community leadership. The life lessons I learned led me to encourage Fanny to document her memoirs, something she had considered but postponed for years due to her incredibly busy schedule.

I met with Fanny on many Saturdays for more than two years. I would pick her up from Shabbat services and then spend time talking over lunch about her experiences. I wanted to understand what personal traits allow someone to survive in the direst of circumstances and then live a productive, full, normal, and happy life. I learned so much more.

I learned about strength and perseverance, resilience, caring for others, faith, love, overcoming hate, commitment to community, work ethic, taking responsibility, accepting obligations, and passing on values to future generations through personal example and stories. I learned about miracles and secrets.

In addition, I learned about Fanny's life in Latvia and later in South Africa, the Nazi reign of terror, Zionism, Judaism and Jewish values, and instilling, as the matriarch, the finest life-enhancing qualities in her family in the United States. I witnessed Fanny's tears and joy in relating her philosophies and experiences to schoolchildren, corporate executives, and military personnel and in peace protests, TV interviews, news coverage, community gatherings, and personal discussions.

Fanny took personal responsibility for ensuring the survival of herself, her sister Jenny, and others during the darkest of days. Later, her focus was on her spouse, her family, and her community and charitable involvements. Fanny's moral fiber is evident—from entrenching her family with Jewish values, to her kindness and concern for others, to her honesty, integrity, and personal conduct. She assumed communal responsibility by committing herself to sharing her story to ensure the world never forgets, and hopefully never repeats, the atrocities she witnessed.

Fanny has always maintained an incredibly positive outlook driven by hope and belief. Her understanding that we are accountable ultimately to a higher power is inspiring and worthy of imitation.

With an energy level exceeding that of most thirty-year-olds—along with her keen intelligence and sense of humor—Fanny is an absolute joy to be around. But even more impressive is her unique ability to make everyone she meets a better person for knowing her.

I trust the readers of Fanny's memoirs will be fascinated, horrified, uplifted, and enlightened by her experiences. Her strength and tenacity, commitment to her faith and Israel, and her influence on four generations of her family are admirable.

It is said, "Never underestimate the importance of having someone in your life who makes you want to be a better person." Through Fanny, I am a better person. Hopefully, others reading about Fanny will have the same experience.

Selwyn Isakow,[1]

La Jolla, California

---

1   Selwyn Isakow has held leadership positions in business and communal affairs. He is chairman of CalPrivate Bank, The Oxford Investment Group, and City of Hope. He is committed to building a cohesive, vibrant, and sustainable San Diego Jewish community through education and other meaningful experiences. He is co-founder of Shabbat San Diego and Partners in Torah San Diego.

CHAPTER ONE

Why Now?

You cannot escape the responsibility
of tomorrow by evading it today.
—ABRAHAM LINCOLN

Invariably, the same question has been raised over and over. At schools, civic organizations, social events, and places of worship, they all want to know, "Fanny, when are you going to write a book?"

It's not like I hadn't thought about it. In fact, the idea had crossed my mind many times. Sure, I had made notes and prepared speeches about my experiences, but I felt I wasn't ready. I felt I wasn't organized. Besides, parts of my life have been, and are still, very painful to recollect. One day, I thought, I'd get around to it.

Well, I just couldn't put it off any longer. When you're ninety-five years old, you've got to think in those terms.

But let's go back to where the seeds of this story were first planted.

In my lifetime, I have visited Israel thirty-five times, beginning with my first trip in 1958 and up until my most recent journey in 2012 to celebrate my ninetieth birthday.

That first visit was a magical experience. You often hear stories of people falling to their knees to kiss the ground upon arriving in Israel. My reaction was similar, yet different—I cried tears of joy. During the celebration at Ramat Gan Stadium in Tel Aviv to mark the tenth anniversary of the State of Israel, I wept. The joy of seeing an independent state of Israel after two thousand years was overwhelming.

As powerful as that occasion was, it was a trip to the Holy Land more than two decades later that truly changed the course of my life.

When I visited the Western Wall in Jerusalem in 1981—along with five thousand other survivors—for the first World Gathering of Holocaust Survivors, we made a pledge: "The Holocaust will never happen again."

It was an extremely emotional moment as we greeted each other at this gathering. Surrounded and supported by other Holocaust survivors, I was encouraged to tell my story and detail my experiences during my incarceration. We didn't share stories with each other, but we were very happy to be together and reunited. Nevertheless, it was happiness mixed with sadness and tears.

Memorial to the Jewish Soldiers at Yad Vashem Jerusalem with six blocks commemorating the six million Jews who perished in the Holocaust

Our mission was clear: to serve notice to the world that the Holocaust must never be forgotten and must never be repeated. We reaffirmed the continuity and survival of the Jewish people with the State of Israel as the focus of Jewish life. And we stood before the world as witnesses to the horrors of the Holocaust through which we had lived.

From a personal standpoint, I had all but made up my mind to come forward with my story. A return visit to Jerusalem four years later only strengthened this notion. At the World Assembly to Commemorate 40 Years Since the Defeat of Nazi Germany and Its Satellites in May 1985, the fifteen hundred survivors who attended, including myself, vowed to share our stories of the Holocaust as broadly as possible. Forty years since my liberation, it was time to tell my story.

On that 1985 trip, I was accompanied by my husband Morris, who had fought in World War II. Along with fellow Holocaust survivors, we walked through the streets of Jerusalem in a parade-like setting. There were flags from each military unit, and the streets were lined with cheering crowds. They were shouting, clapping, and throwing flowers. It was quite a spectacle!

To observe this occasion in Israel was extra special because I'm a Zionist and have been for a very long time. It was double joy.

Then we visited the Memorial to the Jewish Soldiers designed by Bernie Fink at Yad Vashem Jerusalem. Being there with Morrie, a US veteran, was very special. The monument was dedicated to the million and a half Jewish soldiers, ghetto fighters, partisans, and soldiers of the Allied forces who fought against Nazi Germany. The monument, which had just been erected, was assembled in such a manner that six stone blocks representing the six million Jews murdered by the Nazis formed the shape of the Star of David, symbolizing the Jewish people, with a stainless steel sword through the middle embodying the fight against the Nazis. It was very touching.

Up until then, I had been reluctant to share any details of my Holocaust experience, even with my children. I wanted to spare them all the pain that I had suffered. I didn't want to expose them to all the tragedies that occurred during the war. It took that trip to Israel—which my family knew was connected to the Holocaust—to convince me to come forward with my story.

Morrie in his U.S. Navy uniform

By the time they were in their mid-twenties, my children began hearing select vignettes about what had happened to me and my sister during the time we were incarcerated. Of course, they were horrified by the little they heard. Quite honestly, I didn't want to talk about it much. To constantly recall the events that had occurred and the number of lives that had been lost was very painful. So I tried my best to avoid the subject, and my kids respected my wishes.

The war years were never discussed in the South African home I shared with my late husband, Louis, and our three children. It seemed inappropriate for me to talk about my past and, as parents, we did our best to protect the *kinderlach* (a Yiddish term for "children") from sadness and unpleasant events. My job was to provide a normal household and be a loving and caring mother and wife. It was not to cause pain.

I did mention some of the bare basics of my war-era experience to my children after a Holocaust Memorial ceremony in Johannesburg's West Park Cemetery in the mid-1970s. At this ceremony, Louis conducted the choir, which included our sons, Harold and Milton. The ceremony took place next to a monument that had been created by renowned sculptor Herman Wald and consisted of six shofars, or ram's-horn trumpets, representing the six million Jews who perished during the war.

Herman Wald's Holocaust Memorial sculpture at West Park Cemetery, Johannesburg

Ultimately, I realized I had an obligation. If I didn't provide an account of what I experienced and didn't describe the inhumane acts committed by the Nazis, I would be doing a disservice. Did the Nazis think we weren't made out of flesh and blood? Most of us even spoke the same language. I knew it was my obligation to tell everything—to tell the world that it must never happen again.

Fortunately, I've been able to overcome this horrific period in my life. Without question, I've experienced tragedy at its most devastating level, but I have been able to lean on the love, faith, and foundation of family to prevail. The Jewish values that were ingrained in me by my parents—the same values that I have passed along to my own family—have enabled me to enjoy a wonderful and fulfilling life of ninety-five years and counting. I've been able to start over three times—after liberation in Europe, a subsequent move to South Africa, and finally relocation to America. And I've had the good fortune of being able to share incredible experiences and accomplishments with my amazing family and friends. I'm very grateful for all of life's gifts.

Since that defining trip to Israel in 1985, one of my life purposes has been to share my story with schoolchildren, college students, organizations, and the military, Jews and non-Jews alike. I've had an opportunity to talk about my experiences and share life lessons while reinforcing a common theme of "to remember, never to forget."

At the same time, it's my hope and desire to ensure that my grandchildren's grandchildren and future generations understand the atrocities the Jews experienced, the importance of Israel, the values we should live by, and the faith we should exhibit in order to ensure Jewish continuity.

That said, if my good friend Selwyn Isakow hadn't encouraged and motivated me to write this book, I don't know if I would have pursued it. I'm glad I listened to him.

I have tried to recall dates, events, and specifics as best I can. I emerged from the Holocaust with no documents, no notes, no photographs, no clothes, no other worldly possessions. Whatever prewar photos are included here have been kindly sent to me by relatives and friends with whom my parents communicated in earlier times.

Painful memories don't go away, and they don't vanish. They fade somewhat, but the scars remain. It's not easy to forget.

But life goes on, and we have responsibilities. A responsibility to make the most of our circumstance. A responsibility to live and let live. A responsibility to love. A responsibility to build families that reflect the best of the values we have learned from our experiences. A responsibility to assist others to meet their goals and to strengthen the communities we care about. And a responsibility to leave this world having done everything possible to make a difference for those left behind.

I've always said that I'll keep talking about my experiences and lessons I have learned because I have to do it. It's my obligation. It's my responsibility. After all, when I'm gone, all that will be left will be my story.

CHAPTER TWO

A Blissful Childhood

Energy and persistence conquer all things.
—BENJAMIN FRANKLIN

The roots of my persistence and tenacity can be traced all the way back to my childhood.

I started school early, thanks to some determination and some *chutzpah*, or nerve.

After my maternal grandmother, Liebe, passed away, our family moved into a unit in the apartment building owned by my maternal grandfather, Jacob Gamper. I became fast friends with a non-Jewish girl in the building, who was a year older than me. When she turned six years old, she was eligible to attend the local Catholic school. If she was old enough for school, why not me? When I learned I was too young to attend, I cried and cried.

Eventually, my mother took notice.

She marched over to the Shalom Aleichem Jewish Elementary School and demanded to speak to the teacher. She begged her to admit me into the school.

"Just take my child because she wants to go to school, just like her friend," pleaded my mother.

I wouldn't have been surprised if she also told the teacher that my persistence was driving her crazy!

The teacher was hesitant.

"You can put her in the last row," said my mother.

"Okay, bring her," said the less-than-enthusiastic teacher.

So they put me in the back row, but that was only temporary. Before long, I was sitting in the front row, actively participating with the six-year-olds. I have always liked being involved and being part of the action.

A picturesque seaside community, my hometown of Liepāja is situated on Latvia's rugged west coast. Our family called the city by its German name, Libau. Its beach on the Baltic Sea is quite a tourist destination. At the time, Libau's population of about sixty thousand made it the largest city in the Kurzeme, or Courland, region of Latvia and the second largest in the country after Riga. It is located about 130 miles southwest of Riga.

In my formative years, Libau was a relatively peaceful community. This was in stark contrast to the periods of invasions and upheaval that had afflicted the Courland region for centuries. However, nobody could have envisioned the worst was yet to come.

Libau was founded in 1625 and until 1914 was one of the Russian Empire's main ports on the Baltic Sea. During World War I, Russian and German armies vied for control of Courland, and the German military took control following Russia's Great Retreat of 1915. Baltic Germans began forming provincial councils in the other Latvian provinces to the east of Courland when Russian rule collapsed. In March 1918, Russia's new Bolshevik government formally relinquished control of Courland to Germany.

Map of Latvia

At the same time ethnic Latvians were seeking independence, Latvian nationalists absorbed the Courland duchy into the United Baltic Duchy in September 1918. In November, Latvia proclaimed its independence, and Courland became the least-populous of the five provinces of the newly formed nation of Latvia. Then in December, the German military handed over authority to the pro-German Latvian Provisional Government. By January 1919, much of Courland had been overrun by the Bolsheviks' Latvian Socialist Soviet Republic. But the provisional government, with the aid of German forces, pushed back and took back Courland by April. Throughout the Latvian War of Independence, much of Courland remained a German stronghold. Latvia eventually signed the Treaty of Riga on August 11, 1920, ending the war.

In June 1940, Latvia was occupied by the Soviets, and in one year they accomplished what the Germans failed to do in 700 years: to make Latvians favorably disposed to the Germans. The Soviet deportations of 14,000 people from all over Latvia, including some 1,800 Jews, on June 14, 1941 and the 12,000 Jews who fled to Russia after the German invasion[1] were a perfect gift to the Nazis, as Latvians had been claiming all along that Jews ran the USSR and were responsible for all the evils of Bolshevism.

Then Germany invaded in late June 1941 with unthinkable consequences for the Jews of Latvia. When the war ended in 1945, the Soviets again controlled Latvia.

The eldest child of Hirsh-Lieb "Herman" and Sora-Mena "Sarah" Judelowitz, I was born Feiga-Chasse "Fanny" Judelowitz in Libau on October 27, 1922. Cute and plump, I weighed a healthy ten pounds at birth.

I was born into a very large, extended family. My father was one of nine siblings, while my mother was one of four children. Most had married before World War II and had children. Our extended family comprised more than eighty people.

I had an aptitude for learning. In primary school, I studied Yiddish, Latvian, and Hebrew.

Later, I attended the Chait Gymnasium[2] private school, where I studied German and Latin and chose English, rather than French or Greek, which were the other

Fanny at 3 years old

---

1   Edward Anders, Juris Dubrovskis—Holocaust and Genocide Studies, V17 N1, Spring 2003, p. 115.
2   Gymnasium: a European secondary school that approximates American high school and the early years of college.

options. Both schools I attended taught math, science, and the rest of the curriculum in Latvian.

Fortunately, I had a gift for being able to learn languages, a skill that my parents encouraged and one that has helped me throughout my life.

Libau was a very westernized city with plenty of beauty and culture. Big ocean liners cruised through Libau harbor because the water didn't freeze. When I was a youngster, my parents once rented a boat when I had whooping cough. They said the clean, crisp sea air would help heal me. Sure enough, it did.

Our family spent many weekends at the beach, and we had numerous picnics there. The shoreline was just gorgeous. I can't ever recall seeing any weeds on the beach. The sand was so fine and clean it reminded me of white sugar. People used to search for and collect amber that washed up from the Baltic Sea.

Beyond the wide stretches of fine sand were thick sections of bushes that looked like cubicles. When families arrived at the beach, they would claim one of those areas as their own private cubicle. As there weren't any changing rooms around, we would use the privacy of these natural cubicles to change into our clothes and swimwear.

My father taught me to swim there. Nearby were tennis courts and a resort spa, along with several tree-lined parks, featuring beautiful flower beds and benches where people could relax.

The spa had mineral baths and mud baths that were used for treating rheumatism and other ailments. It was extremely popular among tourists who descended upon Libau in the summer months from all over Europe.

One of the parks near the spa had an amphitheater called the Kurhausgarten, where concerts were presented throughout the summer. The philharmonic orchestra played there. Music was ingrained in me at a very young age.

My parents took me to the opera for the first time when I was just nine years old. I was captivated. Years later when I lived in Sweden, I went to the opera and stood at the back of the balcony. They were the cheapest tickets available and all I could afford. But it was the one luxury I afforded myself. Even today, I attend the opera at every opportunity.

Next to the Kurhausgarten was a canal. In the winter, the canal froze over so we could enjoy ice skating.

We loved to stroll down Lilienfeld and Lindenstrasse, with the beautiful villas of the wealthy, the German tennis courts, and a lake with swans surrounding a Hellenistic structure. We would swim in the sea and eat sandwiches on the beach.

Many local Jews would go to the various bathhouses scattered across the city every Friday afternoon for their weekly bath before Shabbat, the seventh day of the Jewish week and the day of rest and abstention from work in the Jewish tradition. Our family would visit the neighborhood bathhouse more regularly.

Kornstrasse and Grosse Strasse had the expensive stores, most of them owned by Jews. Nearby were cafés where the adults sipped tea and watched people meander down the street. There were many beautiful churches, and the Great Synagogue, in Babylonian style with three cupolas, was a town landmark.

Our life in Libau, in the newly formed Latvia, was comfortable, with great promise for the future. Libau had a wonderful Jewish community. By 1940, the approximately nine thousand[3] Jews in Libau made up roughly 13 percent[4] of the total population.

---

3   Estimates of Jews in Libau range from 7,379 Jews in the 1935 census to 9,000 to 9,500 by survivor recollections.

4   Yidishe Ekonomik, published by the Yivo, I, 1937, p. 195: from IV Quatrieme Recensement de la population en Lettonie, Riga, 1936/37.

With my parents and younger sisters, we lived a happy, middle-class existence with a large, supportive extended family nearby. We were also exposed to plenty of cultural and recreational opportunities.

Fanny, Herman, Sara, Jenny – April 1931

I grew up in what we regarded as an Orthodox home. But we were not strictly observant. We kept kosher, but we did not *daven* (pray), or attend services regularly. In fact, my father's business was open on Shabbat.

However, Shabbat was very important to us. My mother worked with my father at his business during the week, but on Fridays she came home early to make *challah*, a braided egg bread, and a special dinner. Our Polish housekeeper helped my mother maintain a warm and comfortable home even after my mother began working full-time in the family business.

When we were little kids, we consumed a special drink we called *med-vyno* (mead wine) for *Passover*, the Jewish festival that commemorates the liberation of the Israelites from Egyptian slavery. In a big wine barrel, we added hops, sugar, yeast, water, and other ingredients. Several months later, my parents opened the barrel, bottled the wine, and corked it.

And that was the drink that we served at the Passover *seder*, a ritual feast marking the beginning of the Jewish holiday.

We also made our own alcoholic beverage, *med-horilka* (mead vodka), which tasted more like a liqueur. We took cherries, removed the pits with hairpins, and dropped them in a bottle. We added some vodka, covered the top with lint, and fastened it with string. Then we placed the drink on the windowsill to age and served this concoction throughout the year.

Even though we spoke German at home, we always learned the Jewish prayers in Hebrew. I attended Jewish schools and had a good foundation in Jewish studies. Although most of my friends were Jewish, I had a few non-Jewish friends, some who lived in our apartment building.

In Libau, there were poor neighborhoods, middle-class neighborhoods, and wealthy neighborhoods. The apartment house in which we lived was located in a middle-class neighborhood. Our neighborhood wasn't particularly Jewish. In fact, it was quite diverse. As a child, I encountered anti-Semitism. They would call us *zhids*, "dirty Jews" in Russian, quite frequently.

Jenny, grandfather Jacob Gamper and Fanny – 1934

My grandfather Jacob, with whom we lived, used to attend the *beit midrash*, or study hall, across the street from the Great Choral Synagogue twice a day for morning and evening prayers. We called him *Zayde*, the Yiddish term for "grandfather," even though German was his primary language.

The apartment building had two stories. Certain apartments, like ours, contained a third story. There were nine or ten apartments in the building. There was another Jewish family—the Turoks—that lived in the building. Mrs. Turok, who was a seamstress, had three boys. After her husband had left for South Africa, she and her sons moved into the apartment house. The youngest son, Benny, grew up to become an ardent communist, anti-Apartheid activist, and economics professor and represented the African National Congress as a member of parliament in post-Apartheid South Africa.

My grandfather was very good to the Turok boys. On Shabbat, he would take all of us to the harbor to buy us some sweets and ice cream. We really enjoyed it.

After several years, Mr. Turok sent for his family in 1934. Years later, I was reunited with the oldest boy, Hillel, who lived in Cape Town. He was an accomplished architect and coauthor of a classic art book, *Camps Bay: An Illustrated History*. He knew that I had moved to Johannesburg, and when I arrived he sent me a note asking how I was doing. From there, we reconnected. I saw him a couple of times when I visited Cape Town.

Another Jewish family by the name of Libauer lived on our street at Berzu 25-3/4. One of their sons was my age, and we attended the same high school.

Our apartment house at Berzu 23-4 had a large garden with cherry trees, various fruit bushes, and a vegetable garden. There was a hammock tied between the cherry trees. The dining room and some of the bedrooms faced the garden. My bedroom faced the street. Everywhere, it seemed, there were lilac trees. That was my favorite plant because it had a wonderful fragrance. I'll never forget that smell. Whenever I see a lilac tree, it reminds me of my childhood.

I was raised in a complex blend of Jewish, German, and Latvian culture. First and foremost, we were Jewish. The world around us was Latvian. Yet we spoke and lived a Germanic cultural life. Like many Jewish homes, we spoke German, read the local German-language press, and appreciated German intellectualism, science, and arts. But unlike many of the German-speaking Jews in our town, we were not sent to German-language private schools, where assimilation was rampant. We went to Jewish schools and were committed Zionists.

Local politics were also complex. Jews considered the Germans to be the bearers of Western, liberal civilization at the time. Liberalism for Baltic Germans, however, was loyalty to the Czar. The Interior Minister, a Baltic German, anti-Semite named Plehwe, had as his antagonist the liberal, "judenfreundlich" (Jew-friendly) Finance Minister Witte, also a Baltic German, whose second wife was a Jewess.[5]

I had a good life growing up in Libau. There were deep-rooted traditions and values such as family, friendship and fairness, and one could choose one's ideals. The freedom to think and act independently was taken for granted.

My father, Herman, was born July 29, 1894 in Aizpute, a town in western Latvia about twenty-nine miles northeast of Libau. After his older brother died, he became the eldest of nine children. He had three brothers (Harry, Ephraim, and David) and five sisters (Bassa, Rebecca, Fanny, Lena, and Freda).

When World War I broke out, Latvia was a Russian possession. My father was in the Russian army and was captured by the Germans. As a prisoner of war, he was sent to work on a German farm. He worked for a German count and was very fortunate to become a foreman on the farm. There was no language barrier, as my father spoke German and could communicate with the count.

After the war ended in 1918, he returned to Latvia and fought for

---

5   Libau Fragments by Ze'ev Wolf Joffe. Translation of German article "Libausche Fragmente" from *A Town Named Libau*. Translated by Bert Knupp, Bettina Brockerhoff-Macdonald, Randall Kloko, and K. Wolfram Wagner.

the liberation and recognition of Latvia. Latvia declared independence on November 18, 1919.

Two of my father's brothers emigrated before World War II. Uncle Harry Lowitz left for the United States in 1923. Later, my uncle Ephraim Lovitt left Latvia but was unable to enter the US. This was based on the high demand for Latvian immigration visas and restrictive quota of about 254 people per year under the US Immigration Act of 1923. Uncle Ephraim ended up in Cuba, which was not an uncommon occurrence in the 1930s and 1940s. A linguist who spoke many languages, he was a translator for an ambassador while in living in Cuba. After several years, he was able to immigrate to the US.

Father's family (left to right): David, Lena, Hillel, grandmother Bella, Fanny, Frieda, Ephraim and grandfather Daniel. (Missing were Rebecca, Herman, and Bessa)

My father provided well for our family as a skilled patternmaker of "shoe uppers" and owner of a retail shoe shop and a small shoe factory. He drew very well, and his role as a patternmaker was to create a pattern onto a piece of leather, which was then cut out by the shoemaker and assembled by adding leather soles.

An extremely handsome and fit man, my father stood six feet tall. His mother was quite tall, as was the rest of her family. However, my paternal grandfather was short, and I took after him. I reached all of five feet two and a half inches, about the same height as my sister Jenny.

My father was also very athletic. A strong swimmer, he would swim for miles and miles in the Baltic Sea.

I had a very warm, loving, and musical family. Evenings at our home were often spent singing and dancing around the piano. My parents had lots of energy, and they created a festive atmosphere in our home. My mother was a talented pianist, while my father loved to joke, sing, and dance. He was a wonderful dancer.

On Friday nights after dinner, my father would say, "Let's dance!"

He would then balance me on his shoes, and we'd glide across the room to the music played by my mother. I felt like a princess in the safety and warmth of my family castle. Love and compassion abounded in our household.

Among Jews, parents seem duty bound by tradition to protect their children from unpleasantness. This was certainly the case in our home. As a result, this loving childhood environment allowed me to grow up with the notion of achieving success professionally and providing for and nurturing a family in a free society with Jewish traditions.

I learned to play piano at an early age on the spinet, a type of small upright piano, in my bedroom. My bedroom was a shrine to my mother's abundant talents. It was decorated with my mother's fantastic embroidery, which adorned much of our family's home. The carpet in my room was hand embroidered by my mother with special wool stitching. It made the room feel more like a sitting room than a child's bedroom.

Meanwhile, the dining room had white linen curtains with magnificent embroidered red roses and green leaves. When my parents purchased a new bedroom suite, my mother created a fine crocheted white silk bedspread. She also made clothes for Jenny and me as we grew up, often identical outfits. She sewed special matching dresses for us for the High Holidays—Rosh Hashanah and Yom Kippur.

My mother, Sarah, was a very wonderful and capable person. Born November 21, 1895, in Libau, my mother was hardworking and loved her family and her extended family. She was so devoted to her father, Jacob. I have fond memories of my maternal grandparents' house. I'll never forget their black sofa with maroon velvet seats. It was very striking. My mother took very good care of my grandfather after my grandmother, Liebe, died and we moved into his apartment house.

My grandmother was tall and attractive. She was also quite heavy. I remember when she fell ill and then passed away. My little sister was named after her.

My mother took wonderful care of me and my sister, Jenny, who was born nearly three years after me. I was twelve years old when our little sister, Liebele, was born. I was overjoyed to have a baby sister.

My mother stood about five foot two and a half inches—roughly the same height as me—and had thick, beautiful auburn hair. Outgoing and personable, she loved being around people. She was also an excellent cook and a talented seamstress.

She was a stay-at-home mom when we were young, but then my father opened a retail shop with a small factory at the back. My mother ran the shop. When we were older, she worked full-time with my father.

My most cherished childhood memories involved gatherings with my family. Spending time with my sister and my parents along with my aunts and cousins was very special. We used to visit my paternal grandmother,

Beila Hirschhorn Judelowitz, on Shabbat morning, and she gave us plenty of sweets—candies and cakes and all sorts of goodies. Unfortunately, over time those pleasant childhood stories faded and were overshadowed by the period of darkness that would soon follow.

My mother had two brothers and a sister. Her younger sister, Yetti, lived in Libau. She had two sons. Uncle Julius Gamper lived in Aizpute, while Uncle Willy, her oldest sibling, lived in Berlin.

Uncle Willy had five children. One time, he drove from Berlin to visit us. It was the first time I had been in a private car. We went on an outing to a town about six miles from Libau. Uncle Willy had to stop the vehicle when I became carsick and threw up in his prized possession. I ruined his upholstery. Motion sickness has bothered me my entire life.

Uncle Willy returned in 1939 with his whole family because life had become unbearable for the Jews of Germany. He settled in Riga, where he thought he could escape the Nazis. Unfortunately, within three years he and his entire family perished at the hands of those from whom he had fled.

Uncle Julius had two sons. Their whole family was also killed by the Nazis.

My middle sister, Scheina "Jenny," was born August 1, 1925, while my baby sister, Liebe "Liebele," was born nearly ten years later, on January 10, 1935. She was just three years old when I left home at sixteen to attend university in Riga. As a result, I didn't get to enjoy her cuteness much. I spent far more time with Jenny, as we were much closer in age.

Jenny and I are the only survivors from the family. She's my best friend. Although we've been apart most of our adult life, I can't think of a world without her. She was a happy-go-lucky child. Growing up, she was my little sister who often annoyed me. We used to chase each other around the dining room table, as siblings often do.

We played in the garden and swung on the hammock that was fastened between two trees. Being the eldest, I was more mature and generally played with kids my own age. We were always good friends, even though we teased each other a lot.

"As a child, Fanny was always reading a book and not interested in playing silly games with me," recalled Jenny.

I remember I would often sneak a Jules Verne book into bed with me. I would hold a flashlight and read the book under the blanket. My mother would catch me reading and scold me: "Give me that flashlight. Enough reading! Go to sleep. You have to go to school early tomorrow."

My youngest sister, Liebele, was beautiful. She was very Aryan looking. She had blond hair and big blue eyes. My mother gave her a great deal of attention because she was the baby of the family. But after my mother started working full-time at the shop, we had a housekeeper who looked after Liebele.

The three Judelowitz sisters looked completely different. I had black hair, Jenny had auburn hair, and Liebele was blond. People now say Jenny looks more like me. When we were younger, that was not the case.

My paternal grandmother Beila grew up in Kuldiga, while my grandfather, Daniel Judelowitz, was born in Aizpute. Both cities were within fifty miles of Libau.

My father's parents had a grocery store and a bakery in Aizpute. They both spoke German and Yiddish but knew and recited the prayers in Hebrew. They kept kosher as well.

Both of my parents' families had lived in the Libau area for as long as anyone could remember.

We used to go to my paternal grandparents' home on Shabbat, and we often dropped by for brunch. My mother used to say that when grandmother Beila made us porridge, she added fresh cream instead of milk so we would put on a little weight. We were so skinny.

We called our grandmother Beila, "omama."

When my own grandchildren had children, they said to me, "Granny, we don't want the children to get confused. What should they call you?"

"I called my grandmother, 'omama,'" I said. "Let them call me 'omi.'"

So, omi it was and still is.

(left to right) Jenny, grandfather Daniel Judelowitz, Fanny, Liebele, and grandmother Beila – 1938

My parents were Zionists and, starting when I was eleven, my teen-age years were dominated by my exposure to Zionism as a member of the Betar Youth Group in Libau. Betar was a Revisionist Party Zionist organization. The organization had a credo that it refused to be silent. Ze'ev Jabotinsky, who founded this worldwide Zionist youth movement in Riga in 1923, once wrote, "Silence is despicable."

Ze'ev Jabotinsky left the mainstream Zionist movement in 1923 due to differences of opinion with its chairman, Chaim Weizmann, and established a new revisionist party called Alliance of Revisionists-Zionists and its youth movement, Betar (a Hebrew acronym for the League of Joseph Trumpeldor).[6] Jabotinsky's new party's objective was the establishment of a modern Jewish state on both banks of the Jordan River[7] with the help of the British Empire.

His philosophy contrasted with that of the socialist-oriented Labor Zionists in that it focused its economic and social policy on the ideals of the Jewish middle class in Europe. He did not embrace authoritarian notions of state authority and its imposition on individual liberty. He said that "every man is a king." He championed the notion of a free press and believed the new Jewish state would protect the rights and interests of minorities. He supported a free market with minimal government intervention but also believed that the "elementary necessities" of the average person, "food, shelter, clothing, the opportunity to educate his children, and medical aid in case of illness," should be supplied by the state.[8]

Comprising mixed groups, along with boys-only and girls-only groups for older teens, Betar activities included Jewish and Zionist education, the movement's ideology, scouting, camping, seminars, work for the Zionist funds, agricultural and vocational skills useful in Palestine, physical fitness training, and preparation for aliyah, immigration to Palestine.

The Betar Youth Group in Libau was led by a charismatic seventeen-year-old *madrich*, or scout leader, by the name of Louis Krashinsky. Louis became committed to the Betar movement in 1933 when he heard Jabotinsky speak in Libau.

---

6   "The Jabotinsky Institute in Israel," *Encyclopaedia Judaica* (Gale Group, 2008 Detroit). Also Israel, History in a Nutshell - Page 71. https://books.google.com/books?isbn=9657542405

7   *My Jewish Learning*, Israel Ministry of Foreign Affairs. https://www.myjewishlearning.com/article/zeev-jabotinsky/

8   Mordechai Kremnitzer and Amir Fuchs, *Ze'ev Jabotinsky on Democracy, Equality, and Individual Rights* (Israel Democracy Institute, 2013) Jerusalem.

The youngest of six children, Louis was very charming and had a wonderful singing voice. His father's family came from Poland and his mother's family was from Courland. His uncle operated a haberdashery business just a few doors down from my father's store.

I attended Betar meetings religiously until I was fifteen years old. Being a member of Betar was a big part of my social, cultural, and religious identity at that time. It was an experience that had a major impact on my life. My commitment to various causes and my philosophies regarding the State of Israel and political leanings were advanced through the Betar movement.

Betar group: Louis (far left) and Fanny in the center (bottom row)

Our Betar group enjoyed lectures, outdoor activities, sing-alongs, and bonfires by the sea. Often, we would gather at the beach, sit on top of an overturned boat, and listen intently as Louis captivated us with his stories. He was a bit older than the rest of us—six years older than me—and I was smitten by his personality and presence.

Louis left Libau to avoid conscription into the Latvian army in 1937. We corresponded occasionally. Then the war came, and we lost touch.

Nursing was a passion as well as an occupation for me. I had originally wanted to become a doctor, so being able to help people as a nurse was the next best thing. Taking charge and assisting others came naturally to me.

I was an attractive and confident young woman when I completed my high school studies at Chait Gymnasium at the age of sixteen. Clad in a light-gray fur coat with matching hat and muffs and wearing stylish shoes designed by my father, I left Libau after graduation in 1938 to study medicine at the University of Riga.

My father traveled with me to Riga. I constantly suffered from tonsillitis, and shortly after arriving in Riga, I needed to have my tonsils removed. It was rare in those days.

I rented a room from a Jewish family in Riga. I barely saw them because I spent so much time studying in school.

In Libau – 1938

The war broke out in September 1939, and it was frightening being away from my family. As I didn't have any relatives in Riga and my parents' business had been nationalized by the communist Russians, they thought it would be prudent that I return home. My mother urged me to enroll in a shorter course at the Red Cross nursing school in Riga. I didn't know at the time that my mother had worked as a nurse during World War I.

Little did I know that the skills I acquired in nursing school would shape my life and indeed allow me—and others I took responsibility for—to survive the horrors of the Holocaust. Through circumstance, my perseverance, street smarts, leadership, and compassion would become, in later years, the basis for building a successful business in a distant country while nurturing a family that continues my legacy.

And little did I know that I would be continuing my mother's compassionate work from World War I. At the outbreak of World War I, my mother was studying piano at a conservatory in Russia. She was forced to discontinue her studies but remained in Russia during the war to serve as a nurse. After the war, she returned to Libau and married my father in 1920. Who knew I would follow a similar path?

CHAPTER THREE

The Nightmare Begins

I have had dreams and I have had
nightmares, but I have conquered my
nightmares because of my dreams.

—JONAS SALK

At the beginning of the twentieth century, approximately one-quarter of the Jewish population of Libau emigrated from the city, some due to difficulties during World War I and some who were influenced by the newly emerging Zionism and immigrated to Eretz Israel, the Land of Israel.[9]

Some of my father's cousins who were Zionists decided to immigrate to Israel in the 1920s. Single and without family obligations, they felt a strong desire to become pioneers in Israel.

They left Kuldiga for Palestine in 1923–24. They had learned of the

---

9   Yad Vashem (2017). The World Holocaust Remembrance Center.

Third Aliyah, immigration to the British Mandate of Palestine, which started in 1919, in their Zionist discussions in Latvia in the wake of World War I. The Balfour Declaration of November 2, 1917, in which the British government endorsed the establishment of a Jewish homeland in Palestine, together with the British occupation of Palestine and the establishment of the British Mandate, spurred the immigration of Jews from Eastern Europe.

Some of the Hirschhorn family changed their name to Keren Zvi when they settled in Palestine. They were part of the Hechalutz youth movement, in which young people were trained for agricultural settlement in the Land of Israel. Once there, they laid pipes in the desert, built roads, and worked on other infrastructure projects. After the war, my cousins tracked me down through the Red Cross, and I have remained in contact with the family ever since.

Like many of the Jewish immigrants, my father's cousins were ideologically driven pioneers. In spite of immigration quotas established by the British administration, the Jewish population in Palestine reached ninety thousand by 1923.

During the Fourth Aliyah between 1924 and 1929, as immigration quotas of the United States restricted the entry of Jews, another nearly eighty-two thousand Jews arrived in Palestine, many because of anti-Semitism in Poland. About a quarter of these immigrants later left the country, but my relatives have remained in the holy land ever since their arrival.

Many eastern European and Baltic Jews saw the threatening clouds of Nazism and communism forming in the 1930s and left their families to explore new worlds—the United States, Canada, Mexico, South America, South Africa, Australia and, for some, the promise of Palestine.

Like the rest of the world, Latvia suffered through the economic depression of that decade. As a result, many people grew disillusioned with democracy, and right-wing groups began to flourish. In 1933, *Pērkoņkrust* ("Cross of Thunder") Nazis started attacking Jews from their headquarters on the Weidenstrasse and the Artists' Cellar on Rozu Laukums in Libau, where Jews had lived in peace with their gentile neighbors. In 1934,

Latvian premier Karlis Ulmanis declared a state of emergency, and the country gradually became a dictatorship.

The thought of leaving Libau in the 1930s was never a consideration for our family. Our situation was quite different. My father had an established business in Libau, along with a wife and three daughters. It wasn't the time to contemplate a move. To emigrate would have been difficult and expensive. And my father was a proud Latvian. He wore a *Freiheitskämfer* ("liberation fighter") pin on his suit's lapel, indicating that he had fought for an independent Latvia.

We supported the Jews in Palestine as much as we could in those days. My parents contributed to the Jewish National Fund (JNF) and supported Zionism.

Then World War II broke out on September 1, 1939, when Adolf Hitler orchestrated Germany's invasion of Poland. Everything changed.

On June 17, 1940, while the world was focused on France, where Paris had fallen to Hitler's blitzkrieg, the USSR occupied the three Baltic countries, annexing them a few weeks later.

Latvia, which had been a sovereign state, was now occupied by the USSR.[10] *Thus began a period of enormous turmoil in Latvia. The Soviets, referred to locally as Russians came in, took over the parliament, and dictator Ulmanis resigned as premier.*[11] *He was arrested on July 21, 1940 by Soviet authorities and deported to Russia.*

Everything in Latvia was nationalized. The Russians seized businesses of the affluent, including Jewish businesses. My parents lost their store

---

10   *19 Months in a Cellar: How 11 Jews Eluded Hitler's Henchmen: The Holocaust Diary of Kalman Linkimer 1941–1945*, ed. Edward Anders, trans. by Rebecca Margolis, Anders Press, Burlingame, California p. 3.

11   Kārlis Augusts Vilhelms Ulmanis founded the Latvian Farmers' Union political party and was one of the most prominent Latvian politicians of pre–World War II Latvia. He served as prime minister in several Latvian government administrations from 1918 until 1934, when he dissolved all political parties in a bloodless coup carried out by the army and units of the national guard, the Aizsargi.

and their factory. They took away the keys to the store but gave them back to my dad because he was forced to run the business. All the money that was generated from sales in the store was turned over to the authorities. Meanwhile, my grandfather's apartment house was taken from him. We were allowed to remain in our apartment, but all the rents, including ours, were paid to the authorities. We weren't the bosses anymore.

I returned to Libau at the end of 1940, having taken the course in nursing at the Red Cross school. At eighteen years old, I began working as a nurse at Libau General Hospital and completed my education and training there.

Our Zionist activities had to cease completely. We were scared and anxious when we heard that some people were rounded up because they had belonged to a Zionist movement prior to the Russians entering our town. And so, even before the Germans arrived, my family had already experienced a great deal of hardship and uncertainty.

We thought life was tenuous, not understanding the atrocities that awaited. At one juncture, in late spring 1941, we filled some sacks with clothing and personal belongings and just sat in our apartment waiting for whomever might come and send us off to Siberia, like many other affluent families, Jews and non-Jews alike, had experienced.

It turned out that these actions by the Russians, however unscrupulous, actually saved a lot of Jews from extermination by the Germans. Some of these prisoners, those who survived in Siberia, later returned to Latvia or settled in Israel when the Russians permitted emigration many decades later.

When the Russians invaded Latvia, they were surprised by the abundance of goods in the stores. The Russian soldiers loved to buy watches. Under their shirts, they would wear multiple watches, sometimes leading all the way up to their elbows. Some of the more prominent Russian army personnel brought their wives and girlfriends and purchased beautiful lingerie in Libau. We were always amused when we went to the opera and saw these Russian ladies in their elaborate lingerie, which they wore as though they were fancy gowns.

Some Russians stole chandeliers from people's homes. They waited until the occupants left their homes and then robbed them. There was no recourse for victims of these crimes.

During the Russian occupation, my aunt Rebecca Drabkin, my father's sister, and her fourteen-year-old daughter, Zivja, arrived in Libau from Kharkov in the Ukraine to visit our family.

My uncle, whom I had never met, came home from work one day and said, "Rebecca, I bought you a present." He presented her with two tickets to Libau. Their two older daughters remained with him in the Ukraine. He could never have anticipated that his heartfelt gift, this good deed, would send his wife to her death.

Aunt Rebecca had not seen her parents or siblings since the end of World War I, when the Russian communist government had imposed restrictions on Russians traveling outside the country. It was the first time our family had met Zivja. It was a time for family renewal and celebration. Unfortunately, family togetherness would be short lived.

We carried on as best we could even though the Russians took over our businesses. It was heartbreaking to see my father so upset. My father worked until the time the Germans invaded and started bombing cities in Latvia, including Libau, in June 1941. Some people attempted to avoid the Germans by moving eastward, inland.

The battle for Libau took place from June 23 to June 29. Despite the usual Soviet stories about the heroic defense of the city, in reality the Soviets were desperate to break out of the city and save themselves. In fact, the bravest defenders were the "Worker's Guard," communists of whom a large number were Jews. Libau was the home base for the Red Baltic Fleet and was bombed during the first hours of the war. The military command had no plans for defending the city and the port. Soon, the whole city was under German siege. The Soviet soldiers tried to get rid of their uniforms and leave the city. However, the national partisans were hunting them down too. Those who really resisted were the young cadets of the Infantry War School. As all the attempts of breaking out and counterattacks were thwarted by the Germans, the Russian defense collapsed. In the rush, Soviets sunk all their ships and submarines. On June 29, after chaotic street fighting, Libau was captured by Germany.

The city of Libau was devastated by the bombings. There weren't enough ambulances to bring the injured people to the hospital. Often, I traveled in dilapidated trucks acting as ambulances to retrieve bodies or injured soldiers and civilians from the streets of Libau. At the hospital, we worked forty-eight hours nonstop just taking care of the people who were brought in. Some died, while others were badly injured.

The radio stations of Koenigsberg, Danzig, and Memel broadcast highly inflammatory tirades against the Jews in Latvian, and the Nazis distributed a pamphlet in Latvian to revenge the acts of "the bloodthirsty Jews who have expelled the good sons of the Latvian People to the U.S.S.R." The German occupiers promptly organized a Latvian "Self-Defense" force (Auxiliary Police), to perform police duties and arrest Jews and Communists.[12]

This "Auxiliary Police" was comprised of former Latvian military officers and members of the pre-war Aisargi paramilitary organization of the conservative Farmer's Union who had taken up arms and joined the German occupiers and later, the Pasaizsardziba (Self Defense) armed fanatical Latvian nationalists, who regarded all Jews as supporters of the Soviet system.[13]

The Auxiliary Police were outfitted in uniforms (without insignia) of the former Aizsargi, the original Latvian Home Guard abolished by the Soviets in 1940. Every police precinct was under command of a German. The Auxiliary Police supported the SD (SicherheitsDienst, intelligence service of the Reichssicherheitshauptamt) which was intertwined with the Gestapo and SS, and heavily involved in the Holocaust murders.[14] By mid-July 1941, Latvian Self Defense members were directly involved in the killings and soon provided standing death squads.[15] There were 3,485 Auxiliary Police in the Liepaja district by the end of July 1941.[16]

---

12 *Encyclopedia of Camps and Ghettos*, vol. 2, US Holocaust Memorial Museum (about 2010).

13 Vestermanis, Margers. Local Headquarters Liepaja. War of Extermination edited by Hannes Heer and Klaus Naumann (2000).

14 Correspondence with Edward Anders, June 2018.

15 Vestermanis, Margers p. 231

16 Vestermanis, Margers p. 225. Situation Report of the District Commissar for Courland of 27 August 1941, HAL, 69/1a/17/B1. 106.

On July 5, Korvettenkapitän Brückner issued the first comprehensive anti-Jewish edict, which included the following: all Jews had to wear a yellow marking of at least ten centimeters by ten centimeters on their back and chest; all men age sixteen to sixty-five years had to report for work at 7:00 a.m. daily; Jews could shop from 10:00 a.m. to noon; Jews could only leave their quarters from 10:00 a.m. to noon and from 3:00 p.m. to 5:00 p.m.; Jews were forbidden to attend public events and walk on the seashore; Jews had to leave the sidewalk if they encountered a uniformed German; Jews were forbidden to use any public transportation; all Jewish-owned businesses must have a sign "A Jewish Business" in their window; and Jews must turn in all radios, means of transportation, uniforms, weapons, and typewriters. Those who contravened these orders would be treated most severely, meaning they would be shot.

In their alleged searches for weapons, the fiercely anti-Semitic Latvian Auxiliary Police invaded the "liberal Jews" homes and robbed, beat up, and sometimes killed Jewish inhabitants. Random killings of the Jewish population began shortly after the occupation. Within weeks, hundreds of Jews were killed.[17]

On July 24, more than 1,150 [18] Jewish men between the ages of sixteen and sixty-five were ordered to assemble on the Hauptwachplatz, the Firehouse Square. We believed they were going to be sent to work in labor camps for the Germans. My father, who was about to turn forty-seven, reported along with his brothers and other male relatives. I recall looking out the window and seeing my father and others pushed and shoved on the street and taken away to the plaza. That was the last time I ever saw my wonderful, handsome, kind father. We would never dance, swim, or stroll the streets of our town together again.

We only found out later that after their papers and valuables were taken from them, they were transported to a small fishing port near the

---

17   Various survivor statements at trials, in books and articles and studies by Andrew Ezergailis, Edward Anders, Marg'ers Vestermanis and others.

18   Anders, Edward; Dubrovskis, Juris (2003). "Who Died in the Holocaust? Recovering Names from Official Records." Holocaust and Genocide Studies. Oxford University Press. p. 128.

lighthouse at the entrance of the port or the naval base by the water tower, where they were forced to dig their own mass graves at the beach, undress and place their clothes in a pile, and wait their turn to be shot.

Some were selected to fill the graves with sand and then await their turn to be killed. It was a volunteer Commando of about one hundred fanatical Latvian anti-communists and anti-Semites, organized by the SS and ex-policemen commanded by Viktors Arājs from Riga, who fired the weapons that killed or wounded the men.

Wounded men were buried alive. After complaints from Latvians living near the lighthouse about the noise, future executions were moved to Šķēde.

These operations were part of "the Final Solution to the Jewish Question," Hitler's plan to eradicate Jews from Europe and then the world, and were led by the SS. SS is an abbreviation for Schutzstaffel, which is German for "protective squadron." The SS was formed originally within the German Nazi Party as a bodyguard for Adolf Hitler and other Nazi leaders and led by Heinrich Himmler. However, the SS became the most vicious and feared element of the German military machine.

Herman Judelowitz

At this time, ordinary Latvians who were so inclined took advantage of the beleaguered Jewish population by scheming to extract valuables from desperate families. Weeks after my father was taken away, our laundress—someone whom we regarded as a trusted employee—approached my mother with a proposition.

"Give me your fur coat, and I will exchange it for some food for your husband," she said.

So my mother gladly obliged and gave up the coat along with other valuables—as did many other Jews—to feed her husband. Of course, it was all a ruse and in vain.

Only later did we discover that my father—along with the others—had suffered a gruesome death much earlier. The cruelty was indescribable and unfathomable.

Many Latvians collaborated with the Germans. There was a special brigade comprising former Latvian military personnel who were very anti-Semitic. They did most of the dirty work and brutally murdered the vast majority of Libau's Jewish population. They said they did it because the Germans had ordered them to do so.

From June to December 1941, groups of Jewish women were ordered to work by the SS. They were required to meet on the street in the morning, form columns, and then walk to their designated duties under the watchful eyes of the SS. Some, like my mother, had seamstress responsibilities and would sew or darn any clothing the *Schutzpolizei*, the uniformed police of most cities and large towns, needed repaired. Those qualified to perform other artisan work were allocated to different units managed by the SS. But most women, like my sister Jenny, were ordered to "chop" or "clean" bricks, taking pieces of rubble and forming them into usable bricks. Jenny performed her manual labor duties outdoors for the *Wehrmacht* (German military) at the *Kriegshafen* (naval war port).

The chopped bricks were used by artisans to repair or rebuild the many buildings in Libau that had been damaged or destroyed in the German offensive to take control of the city from the Russians. The pieces of the bricks that could not be used for rebuilding were used to repair railway tracks. This forced labor was difficult, dangerous, and isolating, particularly as the bitter winter arrived. Meanwhile, the men, unless they were qualified to work on the buildings or for the Germans, dug trenches all day long.

As a Jew, I was no longer allowed to work at the Libau General Hospital. Through the good work of the Jewish Council—a respected senior body of two prominent Jews who represented the interests of the remaining Jewish community—the authorities provided a small, inadequately equipped "hospital" only for Jews. Before the occupation, this facility had been called Linas HaTzedek and was patronized by the poorer Jews of Libau.

I worked at Linas HaTzedek, an eight-bed hospital with an emergency room. There were four doctors, along with me and a few support people at the hospital. Staff included Dr. Zik, the surgeon; Dr. Baron, the gynecologist; Dr. Plotkin, another gynecologist; and Dr. Weinreich, a dermatologist. The Germans put Dr. Weinreich in charge of the hospital, and Dr. Zik spent most of his time in the emergency room. The four doctors had previously worked in private practice at the Libau General Hospital or at other nursing homes.

The small medical staff had to provide health services, run the hospital, staff it around the clock, and clean it. There was little medication. There were seldom any penicillin equivalents. There were hardly any instruments. The Germans provided the absolute bare minimum. Occasionally, one of the Germans would feel sorry for us, and we were able to get a few basic things. But in general, we just had to make do with what we had.

Menasch "Monya" Kaganski was chief legal counsel and a leader of the Jewish Council taking care of all the Jewish community needs at the time. He was a well-respected, well-connected, prominent lawyer who studied at the University in Riga and then went to Paris to obtain his Doctor of Laws degree. By the age of thirty-four, he had become a very distinguished lawyer in Libau, with clients from all walks of life.

He would regularly visit Linas HaTzedek to see his good friends, the four doctors with whom I worked. He and I met in 1941 and became good friends and close confidants. He would occasionally walk me home after work at the hospital.

Later in 1941, Monya invited me to his home to meet his parents,

Lew and Betty Kaganski. I had an immediate and strong connection with them. I would become a frequent guest in the Kaganski home. It was clear that Monya and I had become very fond of each other.

On a cold day in September 1941, after murdering most of the Jewish male population, the SS rounded up all the elderly and incapacitated from hospitals and homes.

This raid was conducted on Yom Kippur, no less, the holiest day on the Jewish calendar. The SS ordered the older and disabled Jews, as well as pregnant women, to remain in their dwellings. They told them they would be relocated. While others went to perform their commanded jobs, the SS went from house to house to remove these individuals, who were taken away to the trenches in the neighborhood woods and shot as part of an *Aktion*, an operation involving the mass assembly, deportation, and murder of Jews by the Nazis during the Holocaust. So began the systematic killing of another approximately two thousand Libau Jews.

My paternal grandparents, along with my visiting aunt Rebecca, were among those killed. Rebecca had been told that, if confronted by the Germans, she should just explain that she was Russian. Then she would become a prisoner of war and be spared. But she refused to do so.

"I'm Jewish," she said when the order was announced, not knowing where the Germans would take the elderly. "If my parents and my brother are going, I'm going with them too."

Rebecca put a yellow star on her clothing, which automatically identified her as a Jewess and prey for those hyenas. Who could have imagined anything so horrific could be possible?

The Germans also took my younger cousin Zivja, who looked Russian with her blond hair and light-colored eyes. I thought that was the last I would ever hear of Zivja.

Decades later, I received a letter signed, "Olga, your cousin from

Kharkov." She had changed her name from Zivja. I was shocked when she contacted me to tell me her story. I was certain she had been captured and killed in the raid. But she had claimed to be Russian, and not Jewish, and was able to escape the Germans. While her mother had died along with my grandparents, Olga told me she ran away and hid with righteous gentiles in a town called Grobiņa, about seven miles outside Libau. She found refuge with the Latvians. She later married a non-Jew and converted to Catholicism.

She saw my name on a Holocaust registry and contacted me in America. In her letter, Olga told me she had a son and a daughter and was still living in Grobiņa. She and her daughter visited with Jenny when my sister traveled to Libau in 2004 for a Holocaust memorial service.

Within a few weeks of these killings, my mother and maternal grand-father decided to place what appeared to be a significant amount of cash in a canister and buried it in the apartment's garden. It seemed a logical thing to do: try and salvage something of value for when the war was over and we all returned to our homes and a normal life.

But then came December 15, 1941. It was the first day of *Chanukah*, the festival of lights, the holiday of freedom, when Jews light the first candle of the menorah, beginning an eight-day period celebrating the miracle of the people of Israel's victory over the Seleucids (Syrian-Greeks) in the second century BCE.

The Seleucids ruled the Holy Land and tried to force the people of Israel to accept Greek culture and beliefs instead of believing in God and observing the commands in the Hebrew Bible, the five books of Moses. Against all odds, a small band of faithful Jews, led by Judah the Maccabee, defeated one of the mightiest armies on earth, drove the Greeks from the land, and reclaimed the holy temple in Jerusalem. When the victors sought to rededicate the temple to the service of God by lighting the temple's menorah (the seven-branched candelabrum), they found only a single cruse of olive oil that had escaped contamination by the Greeks.

They lit the menorah, and miraculously, the one-day supply of oil lasted for eight days, until new oil could be prepared under conditions of ritual purity. To commemorate and celebrate these miracles, the festival of Chanukah was instituted. The Hebrew word Chanukah means "dedication," because it celebrates the rededication of the holy temple.

But this first day of Chanukah was devastating for the remaining Jewish population of Libau. Again, the SS ordered everyone to stay in their homes. We were then told by the Latvians to dress warmly, as we were about to be transported to work in distant places. The SS and their compatriots in the Latvian brigade then went around and ordered all Jews to report to the women's prison at 5 Tiesas Strasse.

There was a knock on our door. It was the Latvian police. The inhabitants of our home—me, my mother, my sisters, my maternal grandfather, and my aunt Yetti and her two sons—followed orders and walked to the women's prison. There, we were packed into an overcrowded courtyard. We were ordered to stand in lines facing a wall.

As fate would have it, I happened to be wearing a Red Cross armband on my maroon coat with black fur trim. This was the coat I regularly wore with the yellow star and Red Cross band when I went to work. This was done so I wouldn't be harassed by German militia or SS. They would let me walk unimpeded so I could arrive on time to work in the hospital. I also wore my best handmade boots. We carried our meager belongings for what we were told would be a train ride.

We were apprehensive as our group of eight stood in line. A German SS officer walked up and down the line, selecting those who should go to the left and who should go to the right. Who should live and who should die.

I must have caught the attention of the officer. He stopped in front of me. He pulled me from the line and asked me to accompany him to the office.

When we got there, he asked me how old I was. I told him I was nineteen. Then he asked me about the white armband with the Red Cross and assorted other questions. I confirmed that I was a qualified nurse and answered his remaining questions with respect and trepidation.

"Guard, let her go," the officer barked. I was free to leave the line and go home.

"What about my mother and sisters—my family?" I asked.

"I'm telling you, just you! Now go!" the SS officer shouted.

Conjuring up more strength and courage than I believed I had, I turned around and said, "No. I can't go without my mother and sisters. If you don't let me take them with me, I shall remain here too."

"Leave now and save yourself," replied the infuriated officer.

I stood my ground and repeated that I would not leave without my mother and sisters.

"You're too beautiful to die," said the officer in a stern tone. "Take them with you, and get out!" Then, glaring at me and shouting at the guard at the office door, he added, "Don't ever let me see her again."

So on this late, cold, and snowy night, I grabbed my little sister, my middle sister, and my mother, and we ran from the prison. With much relief, we were spared.

For the four remaining members of my family, it was indeed a Chanukah miracle. But clearly, there was no joy or celebration. We did not light the remaining seven Chanukah candles in 1941.

Unfortunately, we left behind my grandfather, my aunt, and my two little cousins. Tragically, over the next three days, they and approximately three thousand others, predominantly women and children, were taken on

Bodies in mass grave at Škēde

rough sled rides or marched in columns about four miles to Shkeden (Šķēde) beach.

At Šķēde, there was a small barn that was used as a temporary holding point for the victims until their turn came to be executed. A trench had been dug in the dunes that ran parallel to the shore.19 In groups of twenty or so, they were marched closer to the trench, where they were ordered to lie facedown on the ground. Then, in groups of ten, they were made to take off their outer clothing, and as they approached the trench they were ordered to strip completely, eventually standing naked next to the trenches dug by Jewish forced laborers. If they didn't move fast enough, they were whipped.20 Then, facing away from their Latvian killers (under the watchful eye of the German SS), they were shot and fell into the trench. Then it was the turn of the next group to be murdered. Some didn't die from the shooting, and amid shouts of pain and cries for help, they were covered with calcium hypochlorite while sand was shoveled on top of them. Many were buried alive.

The events of December 15, 1941, continue to haunt me to this day, and I'm overcome with guilt that I was unable to save all of my family. All my remaining aunts, uncles, and cousins who lived in other parts of Libau or in nearby towns were also killed in this *Aktion.*

Jewish women awaiting execution at Šķēde

Photographs and film show German troops and some ordinary Latvians standing around and observing this spectacle of mass murder as if it were a sporting event, a mere curiosity. It was later reported that some of the killers could not bear the sight of these killings anymore and literally went crazy.

---

19   Ezergailis, *The Holocaust in Latvia 1941–1944* (The Missing Center, Historical Institute of Latvia [in association with the United States Holocaust Memorial Museum], 1996), p. 293–94.

20   Latvian guard, Bulvāns, testimony regarding whippings by SS-Scharführer ("squad leader"), Karl-Emil Strott and Philip Krapp - Ezergailis 1996, p. 294.

The German commissar named Laze heard about these massacres and asked Berlin either to stop these or change the means of extermination. He argued the killings were disrupting his plans for the work the Jews were carrying out for the German army. The laconic reply he received from Berlin was "economic considerations are not to be taken into account in solving that problem."

Monya and his family had not been picked up by the SS as part of the December 15 roundup of Jews.

When I went to visit Monya after being released from the women's prison, he asked me to deliver a message to a former client of his. The message was that Monya had been forced to move from his apartment and office at 36 Graudu Street, the main street of Libau, which had been taken over by the occupying Germans. He was now living with his mother and father at apartment 7-4 on Tiklo Street and was asking that the residents of this apartment be protected against rumored future "evacuations" of Jews.

Monya had previously represented this client and saved him from being sent to Siberia by the Russians for being a nationalist rather than a communist. The client was now a member of the Aizsargi, and Monya, as one of two members of the respected Jewish Council, had maintained contact with this official.

Monya asked me to go to an address where a party was being held, ask for this person, and give him the message. Scared but determined to fulfill Monya's request, I removed the yellow star from my overcoat, placed a scarf over my head, and made the trip across town as requested. Upon arrival at the address, I gingerly knocked on the door. A butler opened the door, and I asked to speak to the specified person. I was terrified.

A rather large, drunk man then appeared at the door. He abruptly asked what I wanted, and I confidently provided him with the necessary information Monya had given me. I turned around and rushed back home in the dark, alone and frightened. When I reached my family's apartment, I was one exhausted but relieved young woman. Fortunately, I had accomplished the mission for Monya.

After the December 15, 1941, major *Aktion*, Monya asked me to move into his family's home and become his wife. We were frightened by what was happening around us, and we looked to each other for support and comfort.

It was not regarded as respectable for a young woman to move into a home with her companion, even if it was his parents' home. So, in a hurriedly organized informal marriage ceremony at the Kaganski home, Zalman Israelit, the head of the Jewish Council, conducted the simple service with Monya's parents in attendance. Arranging any event was virtually impossible due to all our irregular schedules, which were determined at the spur of the moment by the guards and the Germans. As a result, my mother and sisters, who were at their jobs, were unable to attend. A curtain ring was used to seal the matrimonial vows. All jewelry had been confiscated or used as currency to obtain favors from the local population or authorities.

I married Monya, a man fourteen years older than me, on a cold, gray day in his parents' apartment. We were one of several ghetto marriages, as they were called. We were devoted to each other and every Jew in our community. Monya worked to ease the burden of those around him who found themselves in difficult circumstances—pretty much everyone. The Germans had banned all Jewish community organizations that had previously operated in Libau, except for the Jewish Council (referred to as Judenrat by the Germans), which they used as their communication vehicle within the community. The numerous Judenräte under the Germans had reputations ranging from despicable to noble and selfless. The Libau Judenrat was regarded as notably noble. As a leader of the Jewish

Council, Monya dealt with the psychological and services needs of the community. Meanwhile, I worked to ease the physical pain of those in the community at the ill-equipped hospital.

In early 1942, while working at the tiny hospital, I came down with a terrible stomachache. Dr. Zik examined me and determined that I had appendicitis. I needed to have my appendix removed before it burst and caused peritonitis.[21]

Dr. Zik said he would operate as soon as time permitted, given that we were often overwhelmed with a steady stream of patients. At the hospital, only local anesthesia and Novocain shots were available. During my procedure, each of the other three doctors held down one of my limbs while Dr. Zik leaned on the fourth limb, made the incision, and removed my appendix.

I spent nine days in the hospital recovering, and on the tenth day, the doctors had me back at work, handing them instruments for other surgeries.

---

21   The inflammation of the peritoneum, a silklike membrane that lines the inner abdominal wall and covers the organs within the abdomen; usually caused by a bacterial or fungal infection.

CHAPTER FOUR

Life in the Ghetto

I learned that courage was not the absence
of fear, but the triumph over it. The
brave man is not he who does not feel
afraid, but he who conquers that fear.

—NELSON MANDELA

After the mid-December *Aktion*, it was rumored that the remaining Jews were to be placed in a ghetto rather than murdered. However, Chief of the Security Police Kügler determined that there were too many Jews—between eleven hundred and fifteen hundred—for the planned ghetto, which had a capacity of around eight hundred. Despite Monya and Mr. Israelit's pleadings, Jews began to disappear in small groups.

In July 1942, a Jewish ghetto was created in Libau. The ghetto comprised four town blocks with eleven houses prepared for the inmates by Jews especially selected for their good physical condition. The surviving Jews of Libau—816 people, including 175 males—were removed from their homes and sent to the Libau ghetto.[22] We were guarded closely by the SS. The ghetto was surrounded by barbed wire with signs that warned any Jew leaving the area without permission or approaching the barbed wire would be shot.

Sign at Libau ghetto in German/Latvian reads: All persons trying to leave or enter the ghetto through the barbed wire will be shot on sight

We lived in very tight quarters with as many as eight people in one room. Most people went to work outside the ghetto and returned at night to sleep. Being a nurse, I remained in the ghetto to work. The dentist also stayed and worked in the ghetto. We were guarded by the SS and the Latvians.

In spite of the overcrowded conditions in the ghetto houses, we led an orderly life, which was mostly due to the devotion of Mr. Israelit, the senior Jewish functionary in the town, and Monya.

Families tried to stay together, even if this meant several people in one room of a shared apartment. In my case, it was four to a room— Monya's parents, Monya, and me. My sisters and mother lived with

22   Ezergailis - The Holocaust in Latvia 1941–1944 – The Missing Center, Historical Institute of Latvia (in association with the United States Holocaust Memorial Museum) 1996, p. 304.

another family in a room in one of the other buildings. Ghetto inhabitants received food coupons that enabled them to shop for meager items at specified times.

I remember making a kringle, a pastry in the shape of a pretzel, for Monya's birthday in June. We didn't have birthday cakes. I combined yeast, flour, and other ingredients to make the kringle. It was my mother's recipe. She was a wonderful baker. I wasn't much of a cook or baker, but I was quite pleased that the kringle turned out edible.

In the ghetto, there was a small synagogue, a library, and a small ambulatory clinic, each in its own room in different houses.

Prisoner column being marched to work
– 1942

The four doctors from Linas HaTzedek and I set up a small emergency room in a converted apartment—or the ambulance, as it was called due to its compact size—to serve the needs of the entire ghetto. The ER had just two cots for patients.

Libau ghetto

We couldn't perform any major surgery there, even though we had a surgeon. I was the only nurse, and I had one or two helpers. We had the barest of essential items and worked day and night. There were so few of us, and we had to serve so many.

In addition to treating all types of sicknesses, we treated

the patients who were sent from the ghetto to work for the Germans or at organizations controlled by the Germans and came back injured. Many were forced to work for the local cork fabrication company and other local corporations under difficult and often dangerous circumstances.

Others were sent to work for SS units that organized electricians, carpenters, and other trained skilled workers for special projects. In general, the ghetto inmates were young men and women, along with some middle-aged individuals with skills useful to the Germans. I administered healthcare to less-unhealthy prisoners.

There was another issue the hospital had to deal with. No pregnancies were allowed in the ghetto. If someone became pregnant, the SS would kill the mother and her unborn child, unless she was part of an SS special brigade and her artisan talents were still needed.

There is nothing more holy in the Torah than giving birth to a Jewish child. Jews are told to "be fruitful and multiply" no less than five times in the first book of the Bible. Simplified, Jewish law states that a woman may not have an abortion after the first thirty days of pregnancy unless the mother's health and life are in jeopardy. In the ghetto, it was determined that the SS regulations constituted a life being in jeopardy, and abortion was allowed.

So, with me assisting, the gynecologists performed dilation and curettage (D&C) procedures to abort unborn Jewish children as a humane gesture. Eliminating Jewish souls intentionally was particularly hard on the medical staff, and, for me, it was contrary to my medical training and religious belief system.

After the war, Dr. Weinreich described the time Herberts Cukurs, later known as the Butcher of Riga, visited the Libau ghetto hospital looking for able-bodied men and women hiding in the clinic. Instead, he found a newborn baby hidden by its mother in her bed. He grabbed the baby by its

feet and smashed its head against the wall, breaking its skull and tossing the lifeless body on the floor.[23]

When the ghetto was liquidated, Cukurs spared the lives of Dr. Weinreich and Dr. Zik, who had once been his own physicians, and they were sent to Riga Kaiserwald with the rest of us. Although there were many eyewitnesses to Cukurs's many atrocities in Latvia, he was never tried for his crimes and lived openly in Brazil until he was assassinated in 1965 by the Israeli intelligence service Mossad.

Life in the ghetto was focused on doing our daily chores. I spent long hours at the ambulance, my mother worked as a seamstress, and Jenny chopped bricks. Liebele stayed in the kindergarten with the other little children whose mothers were working for the Germans.

As days passed, we were just hoping that the war would end. Practically daily and under penalty of death, we listened to British or foreign radio services, hoping that some salvation would come our way.

Chaim Faigelman, who had previously owned a radio repair store, built a crude radio receiver, which was hidden in the house in which Monya and I lived. We kept listening to the BBC (British Broadcasting Corporation) and tried to encourage our fellow prisoners not to lose hope, telling them that the end of the war would be coming soon. But of course it didn't.

Just before we left the ghetto, we had to destroy the receiver and eliminate any trace of it, because if the Germans had discovered we had such equipment, we would have been immediately shot.

Monya and Mr. Israelit tried to boost morale on a daily basis. Fellow prisoners judged their own prospects of survival based on these two leaders' facial expressions and demeanor. If they were not positive and smiling, pessimism pervaded the ghetto. If they looked relaxed and smiled, everyone felt better. There was much pressure on the two community elders.

Victims often develop positive feelings toward their captors despite the abuse they encounter. In my case, it was more about recognizing some

---

23   Press, Bernard. *The Murder of the Jews in Latvia 1941–1945*, translated from the German by Laimdota Mazzarins (Northwestern University, Bernard Press, Evanston, Illinois, 2000), p. 145.

humanity in the ghetto commandant, particularly when compared to the inhumane treatment of the other Germans I confronted.

Ghetto commandant Franz Kerscher was not an SS officer. He was a member of the Schutzpolizei des Reiches, which was the state protection police of Nazi Germany and operated more like guards or a police force. Commandant Kerscher regularly visited the emergency room, asked what medications were missing or needed, and engaged in civilized conversations with staff and patients.

This was in stark contrast to the others; with them, giving the wrong response might get you shot. Not that much was ever delivered to the ER, but Commandant Kerscher's demeanor seemed to indicate that he had tried. At least he would occasionally allow me to leave the ghetto in search of sterile materials. Only one Jew disappeared while the ghetto was in place.

The Jewish Council was also active and helpful in the ghetto, doing good deeds for its inhabitants and saving many lives. The Nazi German administration required Jews to form a Judenrat as a self-enforcing intermediary to control the larger Jewish communities across the occupied territories.[24] In Libau, the two-man Jewish Council of Elders acted as the Judenrat.

Unlike in many Polish concentration camps, the small Libau Jewish Council was never required to spy on or undermine their Jewish constituents. The two leaders developed constructive relationships with the authorities and were appreciated by all of us in the ghetto.

At my request, Monya arranged with Kerscher to exempt Jenny from doing hard labor in the cold weather outside the ghetto. Instead, Jenny was put to work in the home of Dr. Fritz Dietrich, the SS and police garrison commander (SS-*Obersturmbannführer* and *Polizeistandortführer*) for the whole city of Libau. This was regarded as a special job to have in the ghetto.

Dietrich and his wife lived in a mansion, and Jenny was required to

---

24   Isaiah Trunk, *Judenrat: the Jewish Councils in Eastern Europe under Nazi Occupation* (New York: Macmillan, 1972).

do their laundry, among other chores. She would return to the ghetto with her fingers bleeding because Mrs. Dietrich would not let her use a washboard. She was forced to use her hands and knuckles to rub the clothing clean. Nonetheless, Jenny was thankful for the job in spite of the manner in which she was treated by the Dietrichs and in knowing the despicable actions of the head of the household.

Police units under Dietrich's command carried out a number of massacres of Jews in Libau, including the *Aktion* of December 15–17, 1941. It was Dietrich who published the order in the newspaper *Kurzemes Vārds* requiring all Jews in the city to remain in their residences. This facilitated the collection and transfer of Jews, including me and my relatives, to the women's prison. From there, they were taken to Šķēde and killed after my sisters, my mother, and I were permitted to leave the prison line.

After the war, Fritz (also known as Emil) Dietrich was arrested and put on trial by an American military tribunal for war crimes, convicted, and sentenced to death by hanging. Amazingly, he was not sentenced for the thousands of Libau Jews he was responsible for killing, but rather for ordering the shooting of seven allied prisoners of war who had parachuted from disabled airplanes.[25] He was executed at Landsberg-am-Lech prison on October 22, 1948.[26]

In addition to the four doctors, I worked with a female dentist, Dr. Ida Isakson, in the Libau ghetto hospital. Her husband and oldest son had been killed after going to the Hauptwachplatz along with my father, Herman, and a thousand other men.

Before she left the Libau ghetto, Dr. Isakson asked me to look after her remaining son, Roma Isakson. It was a promise I kept.

---

25   Ezergailis 1996, p. 296-304. *The Holocaust in Latvia 1941-1944—The Missing Center*. Riga: Historical Institute of Latvia and USMM. ISBN 9984-9054-3-8. United States vs. Fritz Dietrich and others, case nos. 12-1545 and 12-2272 (File US115), summarized in *Nazi Crimes on Trial*.

26   Ernst Klee, Willi Dressen, Volker Riess, eds. (1991). *The Good Old Days: The Holocaust as Seen by Its Perpetrators and Bystanders*, trans. by Deborah Burnstone (New York City: MacMillan), p. 290. ISBN 0-02- 917425-2.

CHAPTER FIVE

From the Ghetto to the Camps

Anyone who destroys a life is considered
by Scripture to have destroyed an entire
world; and anyone who saves a life
is as if he saved an entire world.

—MISHNA SANHEDRIN

The Libau ghetto existed for fifteen months. When it was clear that the ghetto would be closed and inmates moved out, Monya and Mr. Israelit again intervened and pleaded for the inmates to remain in Libau, fearing they would be taken to their deaths. They argued that the Jews were playing a valuable role locally, working for local businesses and providing artisan services to the troops.

They were able to convince Kerscher and a district commissioner official, Dr. Dorffel, both of whom pleaded with the SD and other authorities to let the Jews stay. Dorffel argued that the Jews were absolutely essential to production and would have to be replaced with an equal number of Latvian workers. Kerscher offered to house the Jews at their workplaces if the ghetto buildings were needed for other purposes.[27] These requests were dismissed.

On Friday, October 8, 1943, at 4:00 a.m., the Jews were ordered to gather in the ghetto courtyard. My mother, my sisters, and I, along with Monya and his parents, Roma and Ida Isakson, and all the others in the ghetto were told that we were to be transported to the Riga concentration camp, Kaiserwald. But who could trust what we were told by the SD or the Germans? Others, too, had been collected and told that they were "going to labor camps," only to be sent as far as the Šķēde beaches to dig graves for themselves and fellow Jews.

While we were all hopeful that this time the Germans were telling the truth about our destination, there was great trepidation, despondency, and despair. Of course, none of us knew that Kaiserwald was, in fact, a living hell.

There was little time to pack our meager belongings and no opportunity to go back to our Berzu apartment outside the ghetto and recover our buried canister of cash. In any event, once we had assembled, the Jewish police of the ghetto arrived and, on German orders, forced our group to turn over all our remaining money and valuables, including our watches.

With baggage in hand, we lined up dutifully in columns upon the shouted orders from Kerscher and Hans Baumgartner of the SD. The Jewish police and doctors were separated and sent to another area. There was panic among our weakened, scared group. Speculation took over our minds, particularly among the elderly and hearing impaired, who were confused by the multiple orders. Soon, people were running toward the second area, thinking that they, too, could avoid deportation by staying with the Jewish police and doctors. The Jewish police helped settle

---

27   *19 Months in a Cellar: How 11 Jews Eluded Hitler's Henchmen: The Holocaust Diary of Kalman Linkimer 1941–1945*, ed. Edward Anders, trans. by Rebecca Margolis, p. 57.

everyone down and, under heavy guard of the SD, the column started walking to an unknown fate.

There were mothers carrying crying children, elderly people struggling to stay upright under the weight of their baggage, people collapsing while others picked them up, many throwing their belongings to the side of the street, doing anything so as not to straggle behind and be beaten or shot. The road was littered with suitcases.

When we reached the railway station, we saw the cattle cars waiting for us. We were ordered onto the cars. The steps to enter were high. Many struggled and were pushed by the guards into the cattle cars, each holding forty-five to sixty standing passengers crushed together. Then the Jewish ghetto police and the doctors were loaded onto the cattle cars. We would spend Yom Kippur night, Kol Nidrei, the holiest night of the Jewish calendar, in a cattle car traveling 135 miles for more than twenty hours with no food or water, and not even a bucket for ablutions. It was a deliberate move by the Germans to carry out this act of dehumanization on the most solemn day of the year.

Loading cattle cars for transit to Kaiserwald

It was standing room only in our cattle car, where we were sandwiched shoulder to shoulder. The pain and suffering in these cramped, horrific conditions was relentless. Periods of deathly silence were interrupted by cries of anguish from frightened children and adults. The mood was desperate. Throughout this nightmare, we tried to relieve our discomfort through occasional personal prayer. Many in the group had poison—Veronal, or diethyl barbiturate, a popular sedative—in their pockets so as to avoid an even more horrific death. We later found out that several of our fellow travelers had exercised this option on the train.

Each time the train stopped along the way, it seemed to be in an open area, and panic ensued. It was dark outside. What would happen to us next? When the train moved again, we felt relief, but we were not relieved of our distress, discomfort, and anxiety.

While I held out great hope and belief that I would survive, I was very scared. Like everyone else in the railway car, I could not see outside. And we were exhausted, having been forced to stand throughout the entire ordeal. We were packed like sardines, with nowhere to move. I kept wondering what was going to happen next. Surrounded by young children and older adults struggling through unthinkable conditions, it was hard to fathom that we were being subjected to this inhumane treatment simply because we were Jewish. It seemed impossible, but it was real!

I felt helpless because I couldn't really do anything to assist my fellow prisoners. I wasn't able to use my nursing skills. All I could do was talk to them.

"It won't be much longer," I kept reassuring those immediately around me. "Things will be better soon."

I always tried to focus on the positive. Our life was so stressed and so terrible at this time. I encouraged them to have hope. That was all I could do. I had no means to help them. I just tried to make them more comfortable. We couldn't make any more room unless we pushed someone out of the car.

People were exhausted. Some collapsed like bowling pins struck by a runaway ball. We tried to make each other less uncomfortable, but how could anyone be comfortable in those conditions? Yet deep down I always believed I would survive.

I must have been numb. It is difficult to understand what happens under these circumstances. But the will to survive, to live, is strong. That's what I always felt—not the feeling of death. And I kept telling myself, "I will survive."

We had been on the train since 6:00 a.m. Beaten but not broken, we arrived sometime after 2:00 a.m. on Yom Kippur morning, October 9, 1943. It was dark, and we had no idea where we were. Then the shouting began.

"Get out! Quicker! Damn Jews!" echoed through the night darkness.

We had no idea what would happen to us next.

People were struggling to disembark from the elevated rail cars. SS men with lanterns were chasing us. We were in a forest. Most thought we were being ushered there to be shot. We were lined up and began walking in deep sand. Even though the walk was perhaps just ten or fifteen minutes, it was a struggle. Then we saw a light in the distance and large barracks behind barbed wire.

We were ordered by the SS, the Ukrainian guards, and the Latvian guards to discard our baggage and enter the barracks empty handed. Mothers were pleading with the guards to keep food and necessities for their small children. Their pleas were ignored.

Eight hundred broken and helpless Jews sat down in the barracks in shock. Monya and Mr. Israelit, as leaders of the Libau Judenrat, approached the senior guard and explained who they were and asked what would happen to the group. The German told them they would be organized for work duties and that the elderly and women with small children would be sent to the Riga ghetto until the barracks were readied for them. This calmed the group somewhat. But the children were still crying from hunger. There was absolutely nothing to eat or drink.

We had arrived at Kaiserwald concentration camp in Riga. As the sun rose, reality set in. We stepped into the yard. The camp looked rather empty. What we didn't know was that since November 1941 there had been systematic massacres of Jews in the Riga ghetto.

On November 30, 1941, approximately twelve thousand Latvian Jews and one thousand German Jews transported from Berlin had been marched

*from the ghetto and murdered in the Rumbula forest outside Riga. Then,
on December 8, 1941, approximately twelve thousand more Latvian Jews
from the ghetto were shot at Rumbula. This was followed by the murders in
Biķernieki Forest, near Riga, of Jews recently deported to Latvia from Germany, Austria, Bohemia, and Moravia, referred to as the First Dünamünde
Action. About 1,900 people were killed on March 15, 1942, with another
1,840 killed during the Second Dünamünde Action on March 26, 1942.*

*The victims were lured to their deaths by a false promise that they would
receive easier work at a nonexistent resettlement facility near a neighborhood
in Latvia called Daugavgrīva (Dünamünde). Rather than being transported
to a new facility, they were trucked to the woods north of Riga, shot, and
buried in previously dug mass graves. The elderly, the sick, and children
comprised the bulk of the victims.*

*In 1942, some Jews working at the headquarters of Einsatzkommando
2c were given the task of sorting the clothing and jewelry that had come from
the victims of the massacres in Latvia. Many of these came in suitcases, and
from the names and addresses on the luggage, the Jews charged with sorting
the items could tell where they'd come from. Other personal effects from the
victims came into Riga from all over Latvia where murders were occurring.*

*The local SS picked over the effects before they were sent back to Germa-
ny, and Jewish women who cleaned the apartments of officers found many
valuables, such as drawers full of watches, and closets full of furs with the
labels of their original owners still on them.*

*In the summer of 1943, the Nazis constructed Kaiserwald concentration
camp in a suburb of Riga. There were eight barracks constructed for prisoners,
and the first transfer of ghetto occupants—four hundred Jews—to Kaiserwald
camp began in July 1943.*

In the yard outside the barracks, the SS ordered the men and women
to be separated and to each form a line. They counted the men and asked
them questions such as age and number of children they had. Then they
ordered the men to jog to another barrack, threatening bodily harm to
those not moving fast enough. Next, the women were counted amid

numerous interruptions. It almost appeared there was confusion over what the guards were supposed to do with us.

It was extremely cold in the yard, and the children continued to cry. Eventually, the women were sorted into two groups. Those who were able to work were directed to stand in one line, while the smaller children with their mothers, the elderly, and the sick were ordered to the other line.

Kaiserwald concentration camp

My baby sister, Liebele, who was just eight years old, was sent to the other line. The other line was reserved for those not useful to the SS and would probably result in certain death.

My mother, who was in our line, took my hand and Jenny's hand and asked me to take care of Jenny. Despite our desperate crying and begging, my mother, following her maternal instincts, left our line and joined the other line with her youngest child. She could not leave her eight-year-old daughter to die alone.

"I need to go with her," said my mother. "I can't let my little Liebele go by herself. You two can look after yourselves. Fanny, look after Jenny!"

My mother then ran to join Liebele in the other line.

"Mother, where are you going?" shouted Jenny. And then Jenny fainted.

It was the last time we saw them. They were taken to separate barracks and from there to awaiting trucks.

It was one of the bravest and most courageous acts I had ever witnessed. My mother always put others first, and this was in keeping with her character. She couldn't bear to see her eight-year-old daughter face death on her own. And at the same time, she was signing her own death warrant and essentially appointing me to assume her role as guardian of my younger sister. There isn't a day that I don't think about my mother's selfless act.

The trucks took my mother and baby sister to the Riga ghetto. They perished together on November 2, 1943, when the Riga ghetto was liquidated after its inhabitants were marched twelve miles to the Rumbula forest and shot. This was done to reduce overcrowding in the Kaiserwald camp caused by the closure of the Riga ghetto and to make room for more Jews being brought in from Germany and the west.

At least, this is what I believed for seventy-five years.

In researching this book, we reached out to Edward Anders who was very helpful. He referred us to a chapter written by Riva Zivcon in the book *19 Months in a Cellar*.[28] Riva and her three-year-old daughter, Adinka, had been in the same line as Liebele and my mother after the selection. In her chapter, written about six months after her heroic escape with Adinka, she describes witnessing the tragedy of families torn apart by the selection.

"Heartrending scenes took place," she wrote. "I saw Mrs. (Sarah) Judelowitz say goodbye to her (two older) daughters as the SS men with rifles loaded the unwanted women and their children into trucks to who knows what fate."[29]

Everyone was sure they were being driven to an immediate yet hopefully quick death. Riva goes on to explain that the trucks actually

---

28   *19 Months in a Cellar*, The Holocaust Diary of Kalman Linkimer 1941-1945. Edited by Edward Anders. p. 85.

29   *19 Months in a Cellar*, How 11 Jews Eluded Hitler's Henchman. The Holocaust Diary of Kalman Linkimer 1941-1945. Edited by Edward Anders and translated from Yiddish by Rebecca Margolis. Chapter 9.

transported the "non-useful" women and their children to the Riga ghetto. In the ghetto, the women were sent to work, and the children were looked after by the older women. At least until the next selection.

From emails exchanged with Anders in spring 2018, he explained that based on "the Linkimer Diary" and other sources, there was a major selection in the Riga ghetto in early November 1943 for another transport. It included those Jews from the Libau ghetto who had been deported to Riga on October 8, 1943, and had not been assigned to work in Kaiserwald (this would have included Liebele and my mother). It was at this time that Riva Zivcon excused herself from her mother-in-law to take Adinka to the bathroom. She hid and eventually escaped from the ghetto.

The transport "was comprised mainly of mothers with children. Children under 12 were to be deported to an undisclosed destination (Auschwitz) on that date, and so were mothers who wanted to stay with their children. I learned from the museum curator in Auschwitz that nobody from this transport was registered on arrival at Auschwitz. That meant they were gassed within hours of the train arriving in Auschwitz and never registered in the list of camp prisoners."

Anders goes on to explain that despite some SS men taunting the Jewish women lined up with their children by shouting, "you do not have to go, only the children do… It is very likely Sara-Mene [sic] had stayed with Libe [sic], and so both died together…As far as I know, mothers were not shot in Riga ghetto, as a transport to Auschwitz was already scheduled on November 2 and keeping mothers with the children not only avoided panic scenes, but also used a more efficient killing method. For all their cruelty and brutality, the SS were rational and practical."

Separate sources report that the November 2 train to Auschwitz carried about 360 passengers from the Libau ghetto that had arrived at Kaiserwald on October 8. So I now believe there is a high probability that my dear mother and baby sister were murdered at Auschwitz on either November 2 or 3, 1943.

I cannot put into words the pain I now feel with the reopening of this wound! May their souls rest in peace together.

It was a miracle that Jenny and I were spared that selection day at Kaiserwald. But that joy and relief were overshadowed by the devastating farewell and loss of my mother and baby sister.

"We have to try to survive this," I said to Jenny. "Let's keep ourselves as strong as we can so that we shouldn't be chosen to go to the other side when there's another selection."

For those who weren't in the other line, admission and registration of new prisoners at Kaiserwald by the SS and prison functionaries emphasized humiliation. The men and women were separated into different sections of the camp surrounded by barbed wire. Then an SS man entered the barracks and told the prisoners to surrender their valuables.

Since the SS assumed that the new arrivals had jewelry and money hidden in their body cavities, they ordered medical examinations. This was led by camp doctor SS Sturmbannführer Dr. Krebsbach and SS medical orderly Wisner. [30]

The women were forced to completely undress and pass through a gauntlet of SS men who uttered crude remarks. Wisner often searched in a brutal and degrading manner in every orifice. Within one to three days of arrival, prisoners were led in small groups to register. After we gave all the requested information to a clerk, who noted it on an index card, a number was assigned to each of us. It had to be visible on the prisoner's clothes. My number at Kaiserwald was 7117.

We were ordered to the so-called disinfection showers. In one of the rooms, we had to undress. Then the door opened, and we were confronted by two German SS men with clubs in their hands shouting, "Raus! Raus!" ("Get out! Get out!"). As we entered the next room, others looked desperately for relatives and friends. A guard distributed a bar of soap and asked the prisoners to stand under the showerheads that were

---

30   Testimony of Rita Wasserman, May 8, 1980, and Ruth Rosebloom April 22, 1980.

set into the ceiling. Other former prisoners have written about similar experiences.[31]

After a short time, wet from the showers, we were pushed toward the exit, where we were issued dirty clothing. At the end of this procedure and after registration was completed, the entire block was assembled in the yard, and all were counted again. Then the prisoners learned of their fates. Either you were made to run to a particular prison barrack, or your number was called, and you were loaded onto a waiting truck for transport to a work assignment in one of the satellite forced labor camps.

Jenny and I stayed in Kaiserwald for about a month. However, I did not work as a nurse there. Instead, my sister and I cleaned the houses of the *Schutzpolizei Feldwebel*, the police noncommissioned officers.

We were part of the Kasernierung commando or unit. In general, if you were not part of a commando, you had no idea where or when you were going to work from day to day. Nobody dared ask why, as this could be a prelude to being shot. Kaiserwald was a cruel place, made more so by the presence of *Kapos*—German criminals, many facing life sentences, who were transferred from German prisons to concentration camps to supervise the inmates. Unlike the concentration camps in Poland, where some Jews acted as Kapos, in Kaiserwald there were no Jewish Kapos.

We could never go to work without being watched by Latvian police or the German SS. As we marched in columns after being assigned to work for the day, we were forced to sing German songs. It was so humiliating and heartbreaking, and I still can't stop thinking about it even today. We had to be cheerful. We had to march like soldiers, in step. Otherwise, they would hit us with a stick. While music was and still is a passion of mine, the forced singing cut through me like a knife and continues to haunt me.

The supervision arrangements at Kaiserwald were quite complex. There were the SS forces, the German army soldiers, and the *Schutzpolizei*,

---

31   Angrik, Andrej/Klein, Peter, "Endlösung" in Riga; "Riga-Kaiserwald Concentration Camp," (Wissenschaftliche Buchgesellschaft, Darmstadt, 2006) 393 Reference in Dachau KZ Part 2, Herb Stalpmann, Tuesday, September 4, 2012, http://dachaukz.blogspot.com/2012/09/riga-kaiserwald-concentration-camp-part.html.

and then there were the Kapos. The Kapos were murderers, thieves, and hardened criminals. In fact, reportedly the camp's elder was Reinhold Rosemeier from Hannover, who had been convicted of double murder, sentenced to life in prison, and had already been interned for several years in a German prison before being "freed" to become a Kapo at Kaiserwald. With the Kapos' authority provided by their SS commanders, their treatment of inmates was extremely ruthless and cruel.

Unlike in the ghettos, men and women were separated by barbed wire in the concentration camps. In general, each barrack or block would have its own male or female Kapo.

Every morning started with a whistle or a siren, the signal for inmates to line up outside their barracks and be counted by the Kapos. This roll call was known as an *appell*. We had to quickly get dressed and line up in a row at a certain time. Everyone was given a number. Then they would call out prisoner numbers and assign us different tasks for the day. This drill was conducted several times a day. They would make us line up for what seemed like hours in the freezing cold. That was their sadistic nature.

If we didn't stand straight or the way they wanted us to stand, they would hit us, push us, and kick us. If there were a discrepancy in the count—either someone had escaped or was missing—the remaining prisoners would be severely punished. Sometimes it would be physical punishment, and other times it would be through the removal of "privileges" like food.

The Kapos carried long rubberized batons, truncheons, or billy clubs that were liberally used to strike Jewish inmates with extreme force and ferocity. To add to their sinister persona, the Kapos wore all black—black pants, black tops, and black boots. The Kapos' frustrations from being prisoners themselves combined with their newfound authority over those even less fortunate and resulted in brutality that knew no bounds. They appeared to enjoy hurting other people whom they did not view as fellow human beings.

Worse than that was the repeated and disgusting behavior of both male and female Kapos, who would select individuals to their liking and force them under threat of death to visit the Kapo barracks, where lewd behavior, sexual abuse, and perversion were the norm.

The male Kapos were not permitted to have anything to do with the female Jewish prisoners. But they always found some excuse, some way of making life difficult for you. They were always drinking, which gave them the courage to take advantage of others. There were sexual assaults. Some of the young Jewish prisoners were only too pleased to oblige them in order to avoid their cruelty.

I believe my faith saved me from a terrible episode in which a potential Kapo attacker ended up too drunk to fulfill his intentions. I was one of the fortunate ones who was never sexually abused by any of these terrible Germans.

"God was so good to me," I acknowledged, not knowing what I would have done in the predicament in which I found myself.

Although it was unusual, I did experience occasional gestures of kindness from righteous gentiles. There were two *Schutzpolizei Feldwebels*, noncommissioned officers, whose apartment we were ordered to clean. Each time we cleaned their apartment, we found bread wrapped in newspaper left for us in the wastebasket. It was this bread that fortified and sustained us. Feeding inmates was strictly prohibited, and this act of kindness by the *Feldwebels* could have resulted in serious consequences for all of us, including being shot.

We were so grateful for their kindness. They had to be careful that the other authorities didn't find out. I thought of their bread as manna from heaven. It was a miracle. Not all people are evil. I never believed that all people were evil. I always maintained hope in my mind—and in my heart—that things would get better for Jenny and me and for all the righteous people who assisted us.

Roma Isakson and Jenny Judelowitz met as teenagers. Roma was thirteen years old when he met Jenny, the beautiful, auburn-haired girl with blue eyes, one year his senior.

Even at a young age, Roma was affectionate, caring, and very smart. He came from an accomplished, prominent family. His mother, Ida, and his father, Itzik, a successful herring exporter to Europe and Scandinavia, were highly respected in the local Jewish community. His parents' siblings were all professionals or successful businessmen. Roma was three years younger than his brother, Meier, but the two were inseparable. The Isaksons of Libau were almost aristocratic in lifestyle, with a nanny, chauffeur, and additional help in their home. They were practicing Jews—well educated and intellectual professionals.

On the way to my job at Kaiserwald, I had to walk through a large military garage. One day, I tripped on a steel bar and injured my knee. I was taken to the hospital, where I lay completely vulnerable. Every day, the chief Kapo would come around to check on each patient in the infirmary and inquire as to how long before the patient could return to work.

If the Kapo thought the stay was going to be too lengthy, the patient would be removed and disposed of. No reason to occupy a bed that could be used for someone else who could recuperate quicker and return to work for the Reich.

Of even greater concern to me—as a young female—was the Kapo's sinister personal satisfaction intentions. Each day, when the chief Kapo made his rounds, I would pull the sheets up to just below my eyes, avoiding the gaze of a potential predator.

I remember that frightening day when the Kapo pulled the sheet away from my face.

"Why do you always hide your pretty face?" he asked. "Nothing is going to happen to you. You don't need to worry about anything."

"I do not want to infect anyone," I replied fearfully.

One morning in late 1943 after I left the infirmary, at the usual Kaiserwald roll call I heard my number called. I was being transferred to serve as a nurse at the Riga-Reichsbahn labor camp in Latvia, a satellite camp of Kaiserwald specifically related to the railways. Monya had been transferred to Riga-Reichsbahn a few weeks earlier and had heard they required a nurse for the fifteen hundred forced laborers imprisoned there. He arranged for me and later for Jenny to be transferred there. Roma had moved to Riga-Reichsbahn at the same time as Monya.

CHAPTER SIX

Building Resilience

That which does not kill me,
makes me stronger.

—FRIEDRICH NIETZSCHE

Upon arrival at Riga-Reichsbahn labor camp, I was directed to the medical station, where I met Dr. Kaspari, a German Jew who had been sent there to provide medical services. Dr. Kaspari and I were the only providers for the medical needs of the forced laborers. The prisoners—including Monya, Jenny, and Roma—were required to perform various duties, mainly laying railroad tracks and loading trains with military and troop supplies. Others were assigned to chop bricks, handle electrical work, and perform whatever duties the Germans required. There was no shortage of injuries. Needless to say, we worked long hours.

Dr. Kaspari had a wife and daughter at Riga-Reichsbahn. He was very compassionate and approachable. He was a kind person who could relate much better to everyone because he himself was also incarcerated. Unlike the majority of the prisoners, we didn't have to go outside to work.

The people who worked in the kitchen stayed in the camp as well. Those of us who remained in camp received considerably smaller food rations than those who worked outside. More often than not, they received little pieces of bread or a potato from soldiers guarding the railway lines. But we never complained or asked any questions. If you raised a question, you were either hit or clubbed with a baton.

Compared to Kaiserwald, the living or "existing" conditions at the Riga-Reichsbahn camp were an improvement. Men and women were still separated, but there were no Kapos, no incessant roll calls, and slightly more food. Three-tier bunk beds, or *coyers*, were provided in the gender-separated barracks. These consisted of boards with bags of straw on which inmates could sleep. We had more straw and more blankets than at Kaiserwald. It could get pretty cold in the winter. And we didn't have nearly as many appells as we had experienced at Kaiserwald.

I felt extremely grateful to share a bed with my sister, who arrived at the labor camp about a month after me. But personal hygiene materials were sparse here as well, and even soap was not always available. The food, if you could call it that, was slightly better. Soup, which consisted of potato peels and water, seemed to be served warmer than at Kaiserwald.

While men and women were separated at Riga-Reichsbahn, there were times when they could view each other walking to their respective barracks. But there was absolutely no physical contact at all. Whether you were married or not, it made no difference whatsoever. But everyone was so grateful and very thankful to just be able to see their loved ones one more time.

One morning in July 1944, we were asked to line up, and once again we were sorted, as they called it. The older people went to one side, and the younger ones to the other side. We knew when they took the older people away, we would never see them again. About 350 inmates were exterminated.[32]

The remaining prisoners of the Riga-Reichsbahn camp, including Jenny, Roma, Monya, and me, had our hair completely shorn off. We were completely bald. The women were given little white scarves like handkerchiefs to cover our heads. And we were given new prisoner clothes. Ours were striped with gray and blue or white and blue. You could see them from a mile away. Then we were shuffled onto trucks and taken to the harbor.

On Erev Yom Kippur, the day before the Day of Atonement 1944, we were piled like cattle, only worse, onto a large military transport ship. It wasn't just our labor camp being loaded on the ship, but Jews from labor camps all throughout Latvia. On the ship the men were lodged on the bottom level, and the women on the top one. There were no beds at all. There were so many of us that we were squeezed together, lying on the steel floor. Even on some of the nonsegregated middle decks, it seemed as if there was no room to breathe. Nor were there sufficient facilities such as toilets. You can imagine what the ship looked like—and smelled like—at the end of the three-day journey.

This was the first time I had experienced a journey at sea. And I was desperately suffering from seasickness. Watching so many others also vomiting was indescribable. Eventually I became so sick that I wanted to keep to myself, even though this was a rare opportunity to be near Monya.

We were headed for the Danzig harbor. The Free City of Danzig was a semi-autonomous city-state that existed between 1920 and 1939, consisting of the Baltic Sea port of Danzig (now Gdańsk, Poland) and nearly two hundred towns in the surrounding areas. By 1944, Danzig was not free at all and was under the control of the Nazi Reich.

I had to be assisted off the boat. After disembarkation, we were taken to Stutthof concentration camp, where we were assigned prisoner

---

32   Max Kaufmann, Churbn Lettland: *The Destruction of the Jews of Latvia.* Foreward by George Schwab.
      Translated from German by Laimdota Mazzarins. Edited by Gertrude Schneider and Erhard Roy Wiehn.
      Hartung-Gorre Publishers: Konstanz, Germany. 2010

numbers. My number was 56140. Stutthof was an enormous camp and very intimidating.

Originally, Stutthof was a civilian internment camp under the Danzig police chief, used for the imprisonment of Polish intelligentsia before its subsequent massive expansion. In November 1941, it became a labor education camp administered by the German Security Police. Finally, in January 1942, Stutthof became a regular concentration camp. Stutthof was built in a secluded, wet, and wooded area near the small town of Sztutowo (Stutthof in German).

Stutthof was the first concentration camp outside German borders. In 1943, Stutthof underwent a massive expansion, and a crematorium and gas chamber were added, just in time to start mass executions when Stutthof was included in the Final Solution in June

Stutthof concentration camp entrance

1944. Mobile gas wagons were also used to augment the maximum capacity of the gas chamber (150 people per execution) when needed.

About five hundred Jews made it from Riga-Reichsbahn labor camp to Stutthof. The men were put to work by the Germans to pack produce on trains and build railway tracks, while the women were assigned to chop bricks and stones for use on the railways. Once again, I was assigned to the emergency room.

Our stay in Stutthof lasted only about three or four weeks. Our sleeping quarters were primitive, to say the least. There was no bedding and no straw—just planks. Three or four people slept on a single bunk.

The Stutthof camp system included a vast network of forced-labor subcamps. It is estimated[33] that some 105 Stutthof subcamps were established throughout northern and central Poland.

---

33   *The Holocaust Encyclopedia* is an online encyclopedia, published by the United States Holocaust Memorial Museum, offering detailed information about the Holocaust and the events surrounding it.

In what had become a predictable occurrence, another major development took place on Kol Nidrei—Yom Kippur night—September 26, 1944. Our twelve-hundred-person unit that had previously worked at Riga-Reichsbahn camp—including Jenny, Roma, Monya, and me—was transported by truck 115 miles from Stutthof to Stolp, a major subcamp of the Stutthof concentration camp. Słupsk/Stolp is a city in the Pomeranian Voivodeship, in the northern part of Poland.

Stutthof guard tower

At the Stolp concentration camp, once again the women were mainly assigned to chopping bricks and stones for the railroad, while the majority of the men set the steel rails for the train. Other men unloaded large trucks with military materials to be transferred by rail to the war front as well as supplies for the troops. People in the labor camp were mistreated both physically and psychologically and forced to undertake exhausting work while being subjected to starvation.

The ever-resourceful Roma Isakson took matters into his own hands. As an electrician, he occasionally shorted the electrical system at night. While the Germans scrambled to repair and restore the electricity, he and a few others would raid the guards' kitchen and eat and take as much food as they could, including potato peels. He had conducted several such antics at a few camps, but ceased these activities after he came within seconds of being caught by the authorities at Stolp.

Roma was a survivor by nature. His concentration camp experiences included working as forced labor for the SS, pulling sleds piled with dead Jewish bodies and then washing the bloodstained sleds. While in the Libau ghetto, he was assigned to work for the Gestapo, and that is where he learned the electrical skills that he utilized for the rest of his life and that assisted him in negotiating the gauntlet of Nazi killers.

He was always very intuitive. It was as if he had a sixth sense. Later in life, he shared with his daughter, Sandy, a description of a recurring dream in which he was being sent as a slave to work in a potato field, digging for potatoes. Although in the dream he was desperately starving, he felt he should walk away from his assignment with no potatoes to eat. As he walked away, a bomb fell exactly where he had been standing.

Roma's uncanny instincts had, in fact, played an important part in his survival during the war, as he evaded certain death by knowing when he was in deathly danger and quickly changing his course of action.

I worked as the nurse at Stolp with a Polish doctor, who was a Polish political prisoner sent to the camp for being part of the Polish Nationalist movement and in the resistance. He was one of the Polish intelligentsia. And even though he also was imprisoned by the Germans, he, too, had no sympathy for the Jews. The Poles in general had a lot of hatred toward Jews, which had gone on for centuries.

Unlike my cordial working relationship with Dr. Kaspari at the Riga-Reichsbahn camp, working with the Polish doctor was quite an ordeal. He was very different from Dr. Kaspari. For starters, he was single. He was very good looking and much younger than Dr. Kaspari. He had an Aryan look with blond hair and blue eyes. He was also an unabashed anti-Semite, aside from being an uncaring doctor.

Medications were in short supply. There were generally a few aspirin, iodine and bandages, minimal sterile materials, a little morphine, and some injection shots available. However, it was not nearly enough to treat or heal the injuries that occurred daily among the forced laborers at work outside the camp.

It was the dead of winter, and the Jews—in clogs with no socks—lost toes, fingers, and feet to frostbite. The doctor, with my assistance, would regularly cut off toes and fingers with a woodworking saw, with few calming or numbing medications. He didn't care about making the patient comfortable. He didn't care for others, only himself.

Occasionally, I noticed that injections and morphine had disappeared, even though they were essential for the patients' pain relief. It turned out the doctor was sedating himself and not the patients! After years in prison, he had become a drug addict. And I merely had to stand by and watch the doctor inject himself. It broke my heart knowing that he was depriving some of my patients of the help and the comfort they needed.

Several times, I tried to enlighten him regarding the impact this addiction had on his patients. I implored him to stop diverting medications meant for the people in the camp. He just ignored me.

There were times I had to hide the medication from him or just steal it outright and conceal it in the barracks. Frankly, at times he wasn't "all there" after having injected himself with so many kinds of drugs. I would then give the medications to some of the men and women who needed them.

I did the best I could. We had an outbreak of measles, which is rather dangerous for adults. Yet we didn't have any mortalities or particularly serious, lengthy illnesses. Toothaches were regular complaints, but we seldom had medications to help manage the pain.

The Nazis didn't care. Prisoners were working twelve hours a day here, lugging materials and emptying wagons. And when they returned to the barracks, all they received was some soup, potato peels, a piece of bread, and perhaps a little bit of jam. That would be it for the entire day. If not for the vitamins in the potato peels, we wouldn't have survived. It certainly wasn't much to sustain us.

I was fortunate in that I worked inside the camp, while most of the prisoners went outside to work. So I could have a shower sometimes by myself and keep clean, which kept my spirits up. Every three or four months, I was given a piece of soap. And a piece of soap was like gold.

$\mathscr{I}$ vividly recall the morning when we were ordered to line up, three in a row. Scaffolds had been erected in an open area and transformed into gallows. Three men—a father and son from Libau along with another young man—stood in front of one of the scaffolds.

"These people are not going to be with you anymore," shouted the SS officer. "This cannot be tolerated."

The Germans were making an example of these three men, who had apparently stolen some cigarettes and liquor from a railway truck while out on a work assignment and attempted to exchange them for food.

The rest of us were made to stand in a circle around the gallows and witness the killings. We were forced to walk slowly several times around the hanged men. As a nurse, I felt completely powerless. I could not offer aid to the three men, nor could I console those in the prisoner circle, who had to witness this ghastly event. This was one of the more horrific sights I can remember.

There was a stark divergence in the Nazi regime's treatment of the Jews. A key tenet of Judaism is *B'tzelem Elohim*. That means we humans are all made in God's image, and thus we are required to respect the inherent dignity of every individual, no matter their religion, beliefs, race, or affiliations. I guess if you don't believe in God, there is no reason to act humanely toward fellow beings – to not do unto others what you don't want done to yourself. You set the parameters and just do what you have defined as "right"—politically, socially, and economically.

Between July 1944 and February 1945, eight hundred prisoners were inhumanely murdered by Germans in the railway yard where Jenny had worked laying tracks. Today, a monument honors the memory of those victims.

Other victims of German atrocities included twenty-three Polish children murdered between December 1944 and February 1945 and twenty-three men and one woman murdered by the SS on March 7, 1945, just a day before the Red Army took over the city without any serious resistance. In fear of Soviet reprisals, up to one thousand inhabitants of Stolp committed suicide.[34]

As the war was ending in 1945, with Russian forces moving close to Stolp, the SS tried to remove captives before Allied forces could free them—or before they would be caught red-handed with their starving prisoners. Jenny, Roma, Monya, and I—along with thousands of others—were taken in trucks back to Burggraben, a small town that was part of the greater Danzig area. The camp facility was completely deserted, except for dead bodies of former inmates scattered across the property.

There were no inmates, no bunks, no hay or other materials. Conditions were extremely trying. The two huge rooms were not segregated. Men and women were intermingled. We slept on the dirty floor without any coverings. The food, as in many other camps, consisted of one slice of bread and a bowl of soup daily. Again the soup generally was water boiled with potato peels. No clean water was available to drink. We were becoming weaker and weaker.

They had told us they would be evacuating us from Burggraben. But we waited and waited for seven days. It became apparent this was a transfer point on the way to the Stutthof concentration camp. We were being moved ahead of the surrounding Russian troops who were advancing against the Germans and pushing them back. What is clear to

---

34   Słupsk po wybuchu II wojny światowej; Słupsk po wybuchu II wojny światowej, official city webpage. Beate Lakotta, "Tief vergraben, nicht dran rühren" (in German) (March 5, 2005).

me now is that at a time when they were facing defeat, the German high command was willing to utilize resources not to win the battle but rather to further their Final Solution for the Jews. This was their primary goal.

Russian planes flew overhead from time to time, bombing indiscriminately. We became inured to the bombings around us, having lived through so many other traumas. That was until one morning when I walked out of the barracks as daylight was breaking. I found one of the young girls who had been with us throughout the years in labor camps lying in front of one of the empty barracks. Part of her head was shot off.

Ella Simpson, about twenty years old, was one of Jenny's friends and part of our Betar group in Libau. She was killed on her way to the outhouse during the night. Shrapnel from the bombs dropped by the Russians severed the top of her head and detached one of her arms. This gruesome sight and senseless loss remains with me.

Somehow, only then did I realize we were in the midst of a war zone. We were right in the thick of it. One way or another, the end of the war was near. Whether we were alive or dead, this nightmare would soon be over.

Libau Betar group. Louis in middle with shirtsleeves and tie. Fanny standing immediately behind Louis. Jenny front row far left. Ella Simpson fourth from left in front row.

Ella was not the only one who was killed over the next few days. Dead bodies remained on the ground when we left Burggraben. People we had known for several years. People with whom we had shared our trials and tribulations as prisoners. We didn't know what became of their remains or even if they were buried.

Our group was then ordered on a forced march from Burggraben to Stutthof, twenty-one miles away in East Prussia. We hadn't eaten or had fluids for days. We camped out in the open next to the road. All the time we were marching, the Germans watched us closely, making sure no one escaped. They wouldn't leave us to save themselves. They just urged us—our group of starved, weak, tired, and desperate indigents—to keep moving faster and faster. When you can barely stand up, it's difficult to move faster. Even if you could, you weren't able to push the slower people in the line ahead of you. This went on for several days.

We marched in clogs. In order to keep warm, we wrapped our feet in strips of blankets scrounged from our prior desolate stop. Russian planes strafed the road, and the prisoners were ordered to lie flat on the road or climb into roadside ditches. Many were too weak to climb out of the ditches and were left to die. Others lost one or both clogs and had to walk barefoot or with tattered rags strapped to their feet. Those who were too weak to keep pace were shot on the spot.

Jenny had lost one of her clogs along the way. A fellow prisoner named Telzag took a clog from a deceased male prisoner whose still-warm body had been left on the side of the road and gave it to Jenny. However, the clog was much too large for Jenny. She struggled and eventually decided that her original cloth-covered foot was better than the ill-fitting clog, and she ended up walking most of the way barefoot.

Finally, after enduring this terrible ordeal—walking so many miles for so many days amid Russian planes bombing and shooting incessantly—we arrived at Stutthof for the second time in April 1945. There were hardly any prisoners left in the camp. Stutthof was an extermination camp that had been mainly evacuated. Everyone remaining in Stutthof seemed to be ill. Instead of the tens of thousands in an active camp we witnessed in

Stutthof the first time, there were just several hundred present this time. The camp was a dreadful sight.

As bad as it was the first time, conditions in the camp were now brutal. Without any food or water, people who had survived the forced march were becoming very sick.

We were housed in barracks. They told us to choose one of the cots, which were on three levels. Most were damaged, and some were dilapidated. Jenny and I found one that was more or less intact and chose a middle cot. There was no straw, just boards.

We lay down on the boards. I will never forget what I witnessed next until my dying day. Insects and bugs began dropping like rain from the cot above. It was a horrifying experience. Even though we had suffered through so much already, this infestation seemed over the top. Until then, I'd been able to keep myself relatively clean. There hadn't been a lot of lice in the previous camps. But here we became infested immediately. All of us started showing symptoms of typhus, which is carried by lice. Small red dots appeared on our inner wrists.

We were also getting even weaker. No one was getting any food or water. We were getting nothing. Most people suffered from all kinds of illnesses, like dysentery and diarrhea. And they were dropping like flies. I can remember people standing there, and then, the very next minute, collapsing—dead. Their skeletal bodies were thrown onto carts and taken away.

There wasn't a hospital or equipped infirmary, no place for emergency treatment. All we had was a room where people could lie on the floor. I was again working as a nurse and had to attend to the sick and do what I could. Typhus is a deadly disease unless treated with antibiotics, of which we had none. So many people died, even in the short while we were at Stutthof.

Although I hadn't noticed it on my first visit to Stutthof, the smell and the smoke from the crematorium were quite discernable. Many prisoners died in the typhus epidemic that had swept the camp in the winter of 1944, a repeat of the epidemic of 1942, and their bodies were burned unceremoniously.

Those prisoners whom the SS guards judged too weak or sick to work were gassed in the camp's gas chamber. Camp doctors also executed sick or injured prisoners in the infirmary with lethal injections.

Overall, between September 2, 1939, and May 10, 1945, some one hundred twenty-seven thousand prisoners were registered upon their arrival in the camp. The lowest estimate of victims who died was eighty-five thousand. The real number was certainly much higher, as the inmates who were selected for immediate execution on their arrival were not registered and not included in any accounting for the dead.[35]

One of the most despicable crimes committed by the Nazis was the production of soap made from human corpses of Stutthof inmates.[36]

Professor Rudolf Spanner, an SS officer and "scientist," was owner of a small soap factory located in Danzig. In 1940, he invented a process to produce soap from human fat. This "product" was called R.J.S.—"Reines Judische Fett"—which means "Pure Jewish Fat."[37]

Rudolf Spanner was very proud of his invention. Hundreds of inmates were executed for the "production" of soap. At the liberation, the Allies discovered chambers full of corpses used for the production of soap. After the war, Rudolf Spanner was not arrested and continued his "research."[38]

When the final evacuation of the Stutthof camp system began in January 1945, there were nearly fifty thousand prisoners, the overwhelming majority of them Jews. About five thousand prisoners from Stutthof subcamps were marched to the Baltic Sea coast, forced into the water, and machine gunned. The rest of the prisoners were marched in the direction of Lauenburg in eastern

---

35   "Stutthof, the First Nazi Concentration Camp Outside Germany," JewishGen.org. https://www.jewishgen.org/Forgottencamps/Camps/StutthofEng.html

36   Michael Shermer and Alex Grobman, *Denying History: Who Says the Holocaust Never Happened and Why Do They Say It?* (University of California Press, Oakland, California, 2002), 114–17; "Tests Show That Nazis Used Human Remains to Make Soap," Mail & Guardian Online,

37   Alexander Werth, *Russia at War, 1941–1945* (Dutton, 1964), p. 1019; Auschwitz-Birkenau State Museum, "Human Fat Was Used to Produce Soap in Gdansk during the War" (October 2006). https://www.jewishgen.org/Forgottencamps/Camps/StutthofEng.html

38   "Stutthoff Concentration Camp (Poland)," Forgotten Camps, JewishGen.org.

Germany. They were cut off by advancing Soviet forces. The Germans forced the surviving prisoners back to Stutthof. Marching in severe winter conditions and treated brutally by SS guards, thousands died during the march.

The conditions in Stutthof were abhorrent, and food was scarce. Some desperate inmates resorted to cannibalism. I remember observing three or four inmates huddled around a small fire behind a building. They were cooking something that smelled like flesh but looked more like an internal organ—a human organ. Possibly, it was the liver of a deceased fellow inmate. Yes, cannibalism to survive! In the fight for self-preservation, loss of human dignity leads to animal instincts.

I was bewildered, confused, and shocked over what I had just witnessed. But my emotions were muted by sheer fatigue, concern about those for whom I was responsible, and a general sense that this was just another unbelievable and incomprehensible image in a sea of cruelty, moral degradation, and loss of dignity.

In late April 1945, the remaining prisoners were removed from Stutthof by sea, since Stutthof was completely encircled by Soviet forces. Again, hundreds of prisoners were forced into the sea and shot. More than four thousand were sent by small boat to Germany, some to the Neuengamme concentration camp near Hamburg and some to camps along the Baltic coast. Many drowned along the way.

A floating barge with no operator, full of prisoners left to die, was washed ashore at Klintholm Havn in Denmark on May 5, 1945.

It has been estimated that over twenty-five thousand prisoners died during the evacuation from Stutthof and its subcamps between January 25 and May 9, 1945.[39] The Red Army liberated Stutthof on May 9, 1945. It was the last camp liberated by the Allies. They found about one hundred prisoners who had managed to hide during the final evacuation of the camp. [40]

---

39   Janina Grabowska-Chalka. Museum Stutthof Guide - Historical Information Paperback – 2004. Grabowska, "K. I. Stutthof," p. 66, 90.

40   Janina Grabowska-Chalka. Museum Stutthof Guide - Historical Information Paperback – 2004. Grabowska, "K. I. Stutthof," p. 73–76 and 89–90.

Because I worked in the infirmary, I was not subjected to the earlier death marches out of the camp. On the morning of April 25, 1945, we were given a very hurried order to get ourselves, the hospital staff, and the inmate patients ready to leave the camp.

Those who were too weak to leave Stutthof, including some who were under my care at the hospital, were shot or left to die of starvation.

Both Monya and Roma were very ill with typhus. Jenny was in the early stages of the disease. I had the symptoms of the disease as well, with red dots on my wrists, indicating I was in the three-week incubation period. Nevertheless, I managed to find a stretcher that had been previously used to move dead bodies onto carts to be taken away. We moved Monya onto the stretcher and asked two other prisoners to carry him. Then Jenny and I dragged Roma out of the camp.

Along with about six hundred other survivors of Stutthof, we were taken to Hela, on the Hel Peninsula, the nearest naval port, and then herded onto an ammunitions barge guarded by SS personnel. Only through the limited strength and sheer willpower of the Judelowitz sisters were Roma and Monya able to avoid the fate of the others who couldn't walk.

We were unaware that Roma's mother, Ida, who had been separated from Roma at Kaiserwald, had been murdered in February 1945 in Stutthof. It was two months after her fiftieth birthday and two months before the camp was liberated. It was also about six weeks before Roma returned to Stutthof from Stolp labor camp. Thus, Roma, the family's sole survivor, was left to bravely face the uncertainties of the future along with us.

CHAPTER SEVEN

Rescue and Liberation

Sometimes things have to get
worse before they get better.
—MARILYN FERGUSON

The barge was very primitive. It was filled with fuel, guns, and ammunition. All six hundred of us—weary, exhausted, and sickly—were literally pushed and squeezed onto the boat. The barge was ill-equipped for our transfer to Gotland, Sweden, an island in the Baltic Sea. We had nothing to drink or eat, with virtually no medicine aboard. Nearly everyone on the barge was ill.

We reached the vicinity of our destination in about nine hours. However, the Gotland authorities refused to let the passengers set foot on land because our barge flew a yellow flag, indicating diseased cargo. Many in our group were suffering from the pervasive typhoid fever and typhus disease. This typhoid fever, an acute intestinal infection caused by bacteria and spread by ingesting contaminated food and water, was highly contagious through close contact with someone who was infected.

During World War II, an anti-typhoid vaccine was discovered. However, the Nazis deemed Jews unworthy of receiving it. Typhus, a separate disease caused by overcrowding and poor hygiene, has historically occurred extensively in prisons and wars. There is no vaccine for it. For us, typhus was mainly transferred by lice in our clothing.

Consequently, the nine-hour trip to Gotland turned into nine days and nights of drifting aimlessly on the sea. People died of disease, thirst, and hunger. Some perished from drinking sea water. The sick became delirious, and the bodies of the deceased were wrapped in rags and lowered into the Baltic Sea—their burial ground. There looked to be no way out, and it seemed like death could happen at any moment.

The nine days on the barge were excruciating for Jenny. Her typhus erupted, and she experienced high fevers. She was thirsty and was begging for water. She cried out for Roma and me to give her water from the sea. We refused since people were dying all around us from drinking the salt water provided to them by the SS.

While Roma was getting stronger, Monya's disease was progressing rapidly. I, too, was beginning to feel the effects of the disease. Monya became delirious and, despite not being able to stand upright, never mind walk, started requesting shoes for no reason at all. There was nowhere for him to go. He became more insistent and desperate.

Roma found a pair of tattered shoes that had remained on the barge after their owner had died and been lowered overboard. He placed them on Monya's feet. It seemed to appease him.

Then, on the seventh day of this odyssey, my dear husband Monya passed away. This giant intellect, concerned Jew, and enthusiastic facilitator of Jewish life in Libau was gone.

The dehydrated, withered, and shriveled remains of this remarkably brilliant, even-tempered, highly ethical, and respected man were placed in a dirty, torn blanket brought from the Stutthof camp. When we lowered my husband's body into the Baltic Sea, his final burial ground, my heart sank. But my hope did not die that day.

I shall always remember Monya warmly as a good man. Hardly as a husband, because we spent so little time together, but as a good Jew and a proud one. I will remember him as someone who wanted to live and wanted to see a better life for the Jewish people, for me, for my sister, for himself, and all those around him. My respect for him always was and always will be immense.

Even though Monya and I barely saw each other for most of our marriage and our happiness had been muted by circumstance—the German occupation, the Libau ghetto, Kaiserwald, Burggraben, Stutthof, Stolp, and Stutthof again—we shared a bond that provided us with strength through hope. Hope for a future together, hope for one another's survival, hope for continued and future blissful love.

Victor Frankl best described this phenomenon: *"The salvation of man is through love and in love. I understood how a man who has nothing left in this world still may know bliss, in the contemplation of his beloved. In a position of utter desolation, when man cannot express himself in positive action, when his only achievement may consist of enduring his sufferings in the right way—an honorable way—in such a position man can, through loving contemplation of the image he carries of his beloved, achieve fulfilment."*[41]

Then, too late for Monya, a miracle occurred just when it seemed all hope was lost. On May 4, an Allied plane bombed the SS barge, igniting

---

41   *Man's Search for Meaning*, Victor E. Frankl. Translated by Ilse Lasch, p. 33; describing Frankl's experience in the Auschwitz concentration camp. Boston, Beacon Press, 2006.

a fire. The lowest level of the barge stored military munitions that were covered by straw on which the prisoners sat. The SS personnel frantically attempted to put out the fire before the munitions were ignited, while the guards went to attend to the fire at the back of the barge. The lower level became extremely hot.

Those prisoners who were physically able climbed to the deck by scrambling up an iron staircase. The last few who made it up to the deck had scorched hands and left their flesh on the fiery-hot iron staircase rail. My sister was in crisis, suffering in the worst stage of her typhus. Roma and I were able to pull her up the stairs and onto the deck. By that time, one side of the boat was beginning to slowly sink.

Once on deck, we waved the white head scarves that we had been given when we left the Riga-Reichsbahn camp a year earlier. Boats passed, but none responded. The SS personnel, realizing their own lives were in danger, shot off flares to attract the German fireboats that normally patrolled the area to rescue distressed German ships and personnel. Eventually, a German fireboat pulled alongside the barge and threw over some narrow planks so we could walk from the barge across to the fireboat.

Those concentration camp victims who were strong enough were able to cross. Unfortunately, most were too sick even to attempt to make it across, and some fell off the planks to a drowning death. Amid all the chaos, no one attempted to help those who fell into the water.

Exhibiting all the symptoms of typhus, I still managed to rally and, along with Roma, who was recovering from his sickness, we dragged a sickly Jenny across the planks. Of the six hundred inmates on the barge, just sixty to eighty survived. There were a few from Libau who made it, including Ella Stern, who was badly burned but survived and later lived in New York.

By this time, the SS guards had removed their uniforms and taken the clothes from the dead prisoners in an attempt to hide their identity. We never saw them again.

Ironically, there was a strange kindness displayed by our German rescuers. They gave us courage. They brought us water and hot oatmeal.

They tried to make us comfortable. Food and blankets were distributed to the survivors, and the boat personnel spoke civilly to us, almost as if we were human. This was a welcome surprise after years of being humiliated and treated like savages.

My nursing instincts kicked in immediately. I requested pig's fat from the sailors and swiftly tended to the burns of my fellow prisoners. When the barge was bombed and caught fire, Roma was in the hull. As he ascended the metal staircase and held on to the burning-hot rail as the barge listed, his hands were badly burned. So severe were his burns that after he assisted Jenny onto the German firefighting rescue vessel, his fingernails—which had melted—had to be removed.

The German boat returned us to the Kiel naval yard in Germany on May 5, 1945. To the complete surprise of the barge survivors, many of the ships were flying white flags. We asked them what that meant. They told us the Germans had surrendered.

When we reached land, we were escorted from the boat by German plainclothes policemen who wore cloth armbands emblazoned with *Polizei*. No more SS. Then they sorted the former inmates into two groups—those who were able to take care of themselves and those of us who were too ill to even walk. The really sick were transferred to Kiel hospital. Jenny accompanied me to the hospital.

In addition to being free, I had another ambition. Throughout my incarceration, I had dreamed of sleeping in white sheets again. Weighing a scant fifty-nine pounds and suffering from typhus, I was escorted from the boat to a truck by these plain-clothed men wearing armbands. Along with twenty other women, Jenny and I were driven to the Kiel hospital, where we were placed in quarantine for seven days.

However, we weren't allowed into the hospital wards but were taken into the hospital's filthy coal sheds. For three days—still clad in our prison garb—we slept on old mattresses that had been set on the ground. On the fourth day, my prisoner uniform—which was infested with lice—was stripped off me and then burned. I showered and washed my shaven head for the first time in weeks. Then I was taken to my ward and placed in a bed—with white sheets!

Those on the boat who were not in need of immediate medical attention were transferred to the Neustadt displaced persons camp in Holstein. Others, including Roma, were sent to the Rendsburg displaced persons camp. After our stint in quarantine at Kiel hospital, our group was transferred to recover at a hospital in Schafstedt, a small inland town. For the ambulance ride to Schafstedt, I had no clothes on. They wrapped me in white sheets—like a corpse. Jenny was beside me.

The ambulance had a German driver. On the way, the ambulance pulled to a stop, and I could hear English being spoken, which was not that foreign to me at the time because I had studied English at the Chait Gymnasium. I read and spoke English fairly well.

Then, through a translator, an Englishman asked the ambulance driver, "What is your cargo? Can I see them?"

The ambulance door opened, and I spotted some English soldiers in British uniforms. There was a chaplain, the first British person I met, along with his translator, Michael Neville, a medical student. I was liberated.

I was so ill that I drifted in and out of consciousness. But Jenny, who remained by my side throughout my hospitalization, kept reassuring me.

She relayed to me what the chaplain had said to me in the ambulance: "Don't worry. You are free, and nothing will happen to you."

After assessing my condition, the chaplain and the interpreter followed the ambulance to ensure that I received the appropriate treatment in Schafstedt.

And I definitely did get appropriate treatment. At Schafstedt, we were provided medication and good care, making all twenty-two of us as comfortable as possible as we recovered from disease.

"Please don't die on me!" Jenny kept screaming at me as I lay in a coma initially in the Schafstedt hospital.

Jenny told me later that she cried so hard and prayed so loud for me despite her misgivings about religion. We had been through so much together, and she prayed this was not the time for me to leave her alone. They say there are no atheists in a foxhole.

In a sense, this was a role reversal. Being the older sister, I'd had to look after Jenny all throughout the incarceration. I didn't have time to really think about myself because I saw so much misery around me. And, being a nurse, I had to control myself more than the average person. I had to hold it together and not pull my fellow prisoners further down.

One morning, I opened my eyes and saw my sister. She was so happy that I could talk. She was so happy that I was alive!

"Nothing will happen to you anymore," said Jenny. "You have withstood the crisis, and you are going to be all right."

I was determined to obey her wishes.

I was so thankful for Jenny's support through this ordeal. But I was also extremely grateful to the chaplain and his translator, Michael, who stopped and then followed the ambulance from Kiel. They took care of me. Jenny later told me that when we arrived at the Schafstedt hospital, they met with the doctor who would be attending to me, told him I was very ill, and issued a warning and ultimatum to the medical staff.

"Watch out! There is no reason to let her die," the translator said to the German doctor. "There is enough medication here to help her. She should not be another victim of your regime."

And they did take care of me. From that point on, my health began to improve. It did not take me long to begin to recover.

In August 1945, I was transferred to Itzehoe British Army field hospital, a recuperation and rehabilitation clinic in Germany. Most of

Jenny and Fanny in Itzehoe – August 1945

the girls had recovered, and I was doing much better. The Itzehoe field clinic was located on the Stör, a navigable tributary of the Elbe, about thirty miles northwest of Hamburg.

I was the only one of twenty-two women at the field hospital who spoke English. For that reason, I became the official communicator with the staff. Captain Tom Pritchard of the British Eighth Army was in charge, and I was his interpreter.

Itzehoe British Army field recuperation hospital staff and patients – 1945. Jenny (left) in chair next to Fanny.

Captain Pritchard, a vicar from England, was one of the most caring and considerate individuals Jenny and I had ever met. When he went on a short leave from the Itzehoe field hospital later that summer, he sent us a photo with his wife at the vicarage wishing us well. I still have the photo. Michael Neville, the medical student, was cut from the same cloth. I received a photo of Michael with a few of the recovered girls near the end of our stay at Itzehoe. As a group, we had developed unusual camaraderie and mutual caring. On the back of the photo, Michael had written, "The wonderful days are now coming to an end…" We all had become family. Our only family.

Other survivors found it difficult to maintain their wits, having lost all their loved ones. Not everyone had the *zechut,* meaning "privilege or reward," and the drive to remain alive, even though the first rays of freedom were visible.

We learned that survivors of other barges that landed in Neustadt, Holstein, and Lübeck were greeted by Allied forces who, in pity and with good intentions, fed them excessive amounts of water and food. Many died from dysentery. They had prevailed through unspeakable evil only to be killed with kindness. How tragic!

CHAPTER EIGHT

Recovery

A bridge of silver wings stretches from the
dead ashes of an unforgiving nightmare to
the jeweled vision of a life started anew.

—ABERJHANI

While I was still recuperating and attempting to get my strength back—
and trying to add some weight to my slender frame—Captain Pritchard
approached me with a proposition.

"Fanny, I have a request from UNRRA (the United Nations Relief
and Rehabilitation Administration)," he said. "They want to open a
medical services operation, and you would be the right person to work
for them. Not only are you a nurse, but you speak several languages. You
won't have to practice nursing, but you'll have to provide medical services
for people from displaced persons camps."

"Look, I'm still a patient. I'm still recovering," I replied. "That's my
concern right now."

UNRRA was an international relief agency largely dominated by the United States but representing forty-four nations. Founded in 1943, it became part of the United Nations in 1945 and largely shut down operations in 1947. Its purpose was to "plan, coordinate, administer or arrange for the administration of measures for the relief of victims of war in any area under the control of any of the United Nations through the provision of food, fuel, clothing, shelter and other basic necessities, medical and other essential services."[42]

Captain Pritchard wouldn't take no for an answer. He promised to send a car to pick me up and bring me back to the hospital each day. Still recovering, I accepted the offer and went to work for UNRRA Unit 289 in Germany as a translator and nurse attached to the British Eighth Army, supporting displaced persons needing medical attention. It turned out to be a very interesting phase in my life.

The UNRRA unit consisted of a director from Belgium, a nurse from France and one from Wales, me, and a doctor from Indochina, who had studied in Paris. The doctor didn't know one word of English, and I didn't know any French.

Each night, I would return to the hospital, which was my "office." When I was well enough, Jenny and I were reunited with Roma in Itzehoe, and I continued to fulfill my UNRRA responsibilities.

As an UNRRA employee, I was granted certain privileges. The Germans had to provide me with an apartment. UNRRA supplied me with a car and a tall Polish driver. Jenny lived with me. I earned enough money so that we could make the most of our situation. We entertained our friends at the tiny apartment. We held small parties, including friends like Julio Garbor and his cousin, Andrew Garbor, who were sent from Budapest to concentration camps in 1944. Julio was a film producer, and

---

42   Agreement for United Nations Relief and Rehabilitation Administration, November 9, 1943. Pamphlet No. 4, PILLARS OF PEACE. Documents Pertaining To American Interest In Establishing A Lasting World Peace: January 1941-February 1946. Published by the Book Department, Army Information School, Carlisle Barracks, Pa., May 1946

Andrew was a lawyer. There were many others, all of whom we said goodbye to when we left Itzehoe.

Social gathering at Itzehoe apartment including Fanny, Jenny, Roma, Col. Pritchard, friends Andrew and Julio Gabor, friend Ephri from Libau and several women from the hospital

In my group at UNRRA, I was the only nonmilitary personnel and did not wear a military uniform to work. Nevertheless, I was referred to as Lieutenant while on duty.

At UNRRA, I offered to teach German to Marion Dickens, the nurse from Wales.

"No need, thank you," she replied. "The whole world will be speaking English now."

One day, Captain Pritchard asked me if I had any relatives with whom I'd like to connect.

"I have two uncles in the United States," I said. "I know one lives in New York, but I don't have an address."

"Write a letter, and I'll see what I can do," said Captain Pritchard.

At UNRRA office in Itzehoe

He added that it could help get Jenny and me out of Germany.

Here is the letter I wrote and presented to Captain Pritchard, who arranged for its delivery to the New York Police Department:

Fanny Kaganski (nee Judelowitz)
Statiches Krankenhaus, Bragstrasse,
Itzehoe,
Deutschland
3 July 1945.

Dear Uncle,
I think you'll be happy to hear from us. What has happened to us, you know from the newspapers. Our whole family has been killed except Jenny and me. We are living here in Germany and we are alone in the world. You are the only relation I have and you must help me.

Four years ago, we were imprisoned. Two years in a ghetto and the remainder of the time in concentration camps. On 4th May 1945, we were freed by the British Army in Kiel Harbour. We were ill and they took us to a hospital. We have been here for eight weeks. Now, we are getting better and must soon think about our future. We don't like to go back to Latvia because our memories are so bitter and we don't know what to do.

We don't know your full address and so we give this letter to someone who will help to get it delivered. It is possible that the letter will take some time to get you. Please answer as soon as you receive it. Tell us about yourself and your family and about Uncle Ephraim.

Just before we went into the ghetto, I married an advocate, Monya Kaganski and we were together up until 3rd May this year when he died. Now, Jenny and I are alone with no wish to go back to Latvia where we have so many memories. We hope that it is possible for us to go to you in America but if this cannot be, please tell us quickly because Germany is not a place where we would like to remain and we must find a new life for ourselves as quickly as possible.

Your sister, Aunt Rebecca, and her family were murdered by the Germans in Libau when she came to us for a visit during 1941 and so even our relatives in Russia are no more. There is so much to tell you, but it is difficult to write all at once. When we hear from you and know your address we will write again. Please forgive my bad English. Now goodbye and many kisses for your family from your brother Herman's daughters.

—Fanny and Jenny

Several months later, my aunt, Ruth Lowitz, received a knock at her door. When she answered, a policeman handed her an envelope with her husband's name on it and my letter inside.

"Do you have any relatives in Europe?" asked the policeman.

"Yes," said my aunt.

Before she could open the envelope, the policeman said, "I'm bringing you a letter from two of your nieces."

My aunt reportedly fainted.

Incredibly, my letter—without an address—had found its way to my relatives in America. (Many years later, my aunt presented me with a copy of this letter, reproduced above exactly as written.) The family had given up hope there would be any survivors from their Latvian relatives. My father came from a large family, and we had many cousins, but aside from those living in the US and those who left for Palestine many years before the war, only Jenny and I survived.

Uncle Harry Lowitz wrote back, saying he would do whatever he could for us. He generously sent Jenny and me clothes and thirty dollars each month, enough to make a huge difference to our meagre lifestyle. We even bought fur coats! He also committed to make every effort to get US visas for Jenny and me. He hired lawyers and contacted influential people. But I needed to get to a US embassy to apply for a visa, and at that time, only Switzerland and Sweden, which had remained neutral during the war, had western embassies. Somehow, I had to find a way to get us to Sweden.

UNRRA's headquarters was located in Hamburg. One of my responsibilities was to travel to Hamburg to obtain sterile materials and other medical supplies for distribution to the displaced persons camps.

The road to Hamburg was narrow and wove through many small towns and villages. Driving through one of the villages, I noticed a man with his arm in a sling.

"Stop the car right now," I demanded.

My driver obliged, and I jumped out of the car to confront the man.

"Do you recognize me?" I asked aggressively. "Do you know who I am?"

"You're still alive?" responded Meister der Schutzpolizei Franz Kerscher from the Libau ghetto. "Please don't give me away. Please, please. I have been injured in the war. Please don't give me away!"

He continued to plead for his anonymity, for his freedom. And for my silence. I decided to take the high road. This man, although not SS, was the leader of an organization that had persecuted me and my fellow Jews. His injuries were minor when compared to all those who had suffered mightily or died through his organization's actions. But my ingrained compassion and kindness led me to turn around, walk away, and never say a word about the incident for decades.

There were many times—maybe even most days—while I was incarcerated that I thought about taking revenge at some time in the future, but when the opportunity arose I just couldn't do it. The Jewish value of *tzedek* is more than "justice." It implies compassion, because without compassion, the law itself can generate inequity. Tzedek is a precondition of a decent society.

Several weeks later, on a similar assignment to the UNRRA head-quarters, I noticed a large black limousine with a Swedish flag parked on the side of the road. I asked the chauffeur of the black car who was his passenger.

"I am driving Mr. Wasserman, a Dane who works for an organization in Sweden," said the chauffeur.

I insisted on waiting for Mr. Wasserman. When he eventually returned to his car, I introduced myself, briefly described my situation, and inquired as to whether he could assist me in getting to Sweden to apply for a visa to America. His initial reaction was not encouraging.

I persisted. I told him about my nursing experience and my language skills. He finally relented.

"Perhaps you can work for me as my secretary," said Mr. Wasserman. "But only with Captain Pritchard's approval."

I immediately contacted Captain Pritchard, who gave me his blessing. Then I again met with Mr. Wasserman and insisted that he allow me to be accompanied by my sister Jenny and my adopted brother Roma.

"Difficult," said Mr. Wasserman.

"Then I can't be your secretary," I replied.

However, Mr. Wasserman quickly changed his mind when he realized I could be an asset to him in his search for survivors. His intention was to include the three of us on a transport to Sweden as part of his project mission.

Mr. Wasserman was working with Vaad Ha-Hatzalah, an organization that was originally established to rescue rabbis and yeshiva students during World War II but expanded to assist all Jews. His purpose was to find surviving spouses and family members of previously released prisoners and transport them to their loved ones waiting in Stockholm. These released concentration camp victims were in Sweden as a result of a program established by Folke Bernadotte, Count of Wisborg, a Swedish diplomat and nobleman. Bernadotte had previously negotiated the release of about thirty-one thousand prisoners on April 14, 1945, from various German concentration camps, including 450 Danish Jews from the Theresienstadt camp.

Different organizations, including the Red Cross, had worked to identify these missing relatives and had arranged for some of them to be moved to the Bergen-Belsen displaced persons camp after the war. Mr. Wasserman had a list of names and was searching for any of these survivors for reunification with their family members in Stockholm.

The Bergen-Belsen DP camp was not far from the infamous Bergen-Belsen concentration camp, which was originally established as a prisoner of war camp for Soviet troops and an "exchange camp" where Jewish hostages were held with the intention of exchanging them for German prisoners of war held overseas. The camp later became a concentration and extermination camp and was expanded to accommodate Jews from other concentration camps. From 1941 to 1945, almost twenty thousand Soviet prisoners of war and a further fifty thousand inmates died there.

Overcrowding, lack of food, and poor sanitary conditions caused outbreaks of typhus, tuberculosis, typhoid fever, and dysentery, leading to the deaths of more than thirty-five thousand people shortly before and after the liberation. Upon liberation of the camp on April 15, 1945, British Eleventh Armored Division soldiers discovered approximately sixty thousand prisoners inside, most of them half-starved and seriously ill, and another thirteen thousand corpses lying around the camp unburied.

After the investigation and identification of survivors on Wasserman's list, more than fifteen hundred qualifying people, in addition to Jenny, Roma, and me, were placed on a boat transport from Lübeck to Landskrona, Sweden, in April 1946.

Leaving Lubeck for Sweden – 1946 (left to right): Fanny, Roma and Jenny

Upon arrival, we were quarantined for two weeks. Passover, the festival celebrating Moses and the Jews' exodus from Egypt, took place while we were in quarantine.

One of the survivors identified in Bergen-Belsen and on the boat with us was Mr. Monyak Kaplan, originally from Lodz, Poland. He and his wife, Malvina, were separated early in the war. Malvina was part of a group of more than one thousand women who had been released from a woman's labor camp just before the end of the war in a deal between Heinrich Himmler and Count Bernadotte. It was rumored that Bernadotte exchanged certain materials for this release. Malvina was waiting for her husband in Stockholm.

However, the Kaplans would not spend Passover together in 1946 because Monyak was in quarantine. For those of us quarantined, Monyak and I organized a Passover seder, the feast of unleavened bread celebrating freedom and recalling the trials and tribulations of the Jews leaving bondage and slavery 3,257 years earlier.

Over the years, I have contemplated why we Jews celebrate freedom each Passover, marking our exodus from Egypt and slavery, when in every generation in the 3,330 years since then, Jews have been persecuted, from the King of Persia decreeing death to all Jewish subjects in 356 BCE, to expulsion from England, France, Hungary, Spain, Germany, Austria, and Portugal between 1290 and 1496, to discrimination and atrocities every twenty or so years through the Holocaust and since. I have concluded that one doesn't have to be physically free to be spiritually free to meet his or her responsibility as a Jew. I never felt abandoned when I was in the concentration camps. On those occasions when I wasn't dead tired at the end of a day, I would lie on my uncomfortable bunk and feel free to believe, to contemplate a future, believing that I would have one.

On April 15, 1946, the first night of Passover, Monyak and I, with the assistance and support of Vaad Ha-Hatzalah, celebrated the occasion with *matzos* (unleavened bread), recalling the speed with which the Jews left Egypt, and *gefilte fish* (ground, deboned white fish) from the

United States, marking the group's first Passover in freedom since being incarcerated.

For all of us, there was much to remember and still be thankful for that Passover. The central command or mitzvah of the seder is to retell the story of the exodus of the Jews from Egypt, a story beginning with the despair of bondage and leading to the joy of freedom. A spiritual and physical journey with miracles orchestrated by the Almighty.

Our quarantined group had themselves lived a similar experience, and the meaning of this holiday was not lost. And Count Bernadotte was not forgotten by our group. His interest and efforts in saving Jews was remarkable. He was a man of honor and stature. It was he, in 1945, who had received a German surrender offer from Heinrich Himmler, though the offer was ultimately rejected. Subsequently, Bernadotte was unanimously chosen to be the United Nations Security Council mediator in the Arab-Israeli conflict of 1947–48.

Given all Bernadotte had done for Jews during the war and his determination to forge a lasting peace between the Palestinians and Jews in the formation of a Jewish state, his assassination by the militant Zionist group Lehi while he was pursuing his official duties in Jerusalem in 1948 was all the more senseless.

CHAPTER NINE

Bound for Stockholm

Free at last! Free at last! Thank God
Almighty we are free at last!

—MARTIN LUTHER KING, JR.

The list of new arrivals in quarantine was forwarded to the Stockholm Jewish community. A Rabbi Chasdan, the Vaad Ha-Hatzalah representative in Stockholm, scanned the list and noticed my name on it.

He quickly sent me a telegram.

"Are you, by any chance, the daughter of Herman and Sarah Judelowitz from Libau?" he asked.

"Yes," I replied by return mail.

I then received the most beautiful letter

In Stockholm – 1947

from the rabbi assuring me that we would be welcome in Stockholm and that there would be a job interview waiting for me at the World Jewish Congress when I arrived there.

When I was just a year old, a twenty-one-year-old *shochet*, a kosher animal slaughterer, used to rock me in his arms. Later, this young man fled from Latvia to Sweden and became a rabbi—Rabbi Chasdan.

Like the Judelowitzes, the Chasdans had a bungalow in the 1920s and 1930s in Vaiņode, a village of cottages between Libau and Mažeikiai, which was known as a resort area in Latvia with clean air and beautiful trees where families from the area spent the summer. The two families were friendly with each other.

Nearly twenty-five years later, the rabbi and I were reunited.

Meanwhile, the chairman of the World Jewish Congress in Sweden was Hillel Storch, who had lived in Riga before he left for Sweden just prior to the Russian occupation of Latvia. Storch also had been very active in the release of Jews from concentration camps in 1944 and early 1945. [43]

After our quarantine period in Landskroner, Roma, Jenny, and I arrived in Stockholm. Through these Latvian connections and a successful interview, I was able to land a job as one of the secretaries and interpreters at the World Jewish Congress in Stockholm. The World Jewish Congress provided me with an apartment, which I shared with Roma and Jenny.

These were hectic times for the World Jewish Congress, as it was prior to and during the formation and declaration of the independent state of Israel. In my role at the congress, I wrote letters to many countries lobbying them to vote for the United Nations Resolution Plan for Palestine. Many prominent individuals in the Jewish world came to Stockholm to try to gain support for a yes vote for the State of Israel. Not only

---

43 Storch was instrumental in the rescue of many Jews and non-Jewish Scandinavians from the concentration camps, including the White Busses operation organized by the Swedish Red Cross and the government of Denmark; through negotiations by Count Bernadotte to rescue prisoners from German extermination camps and transport them to Sweden; and saving 7,500 women, of whom at least 2,000 were Jewish, from the Ravensbrück concentration camp, which was exclusively for women, in northern Germany. Storch conducted negotiations with Himmler through Felix Kersten, who was SS commander Heinrich Himmler's personal physician and physical therapist, in the beginning of 1945 that led to Himmler's agreement to hand over concentration camps to the Allied forces in good order and not to bomb the camps as Himmler had planned.

Americans but representatives from many other countries visited our offices.

On one occasion, I received an urgent call at home around 2:00 a.m. asking me to rush down to the office to send a letter to the Danish representative for the United Nations. I got dressed, hustled over to the office, and wrote the letter asking him to please vote yes for the resolution. We needed their vote. Thankfully, that yes vote came through in time.

My duties also included looking for relatives of survivors. I occasionally had an unusual task to perform, such as the time David Ben-Gurion, head of the Jewish Agency, visited Stockholm to attend the Hehalutz[44] convention and didn't have an overcoat for the cold weather. I ran to the store with another colleague to purchase a coat for him.

In Stockholm – 1948

I worked for Miss Hill who had been transferred from the US where she was formerly the secretary for Nahum Goldman, a leader in the US Zionist movement.

I have such vivid and uplifting memories of the night of November 29, 1947 when the "yes" vote by Costa Rica, the casting vote, on Resolution 181 in favor of the establishment of a state for the Jewish people was adopted by the United Nations General Assembly.

I met the most wonderful people at the World Jewish Congress which meant so much to me, especially after what I had experienced. And, of course, the work we were doing was so rewarding. I remember so clear-

---

44   Hehalutz was a Jewish youth movement that trained young people across Europe and the United States during and after World War I for agricultural settlement in the Land of Israel. It became an umbrella organization of the pioneering Zionist youth movements.

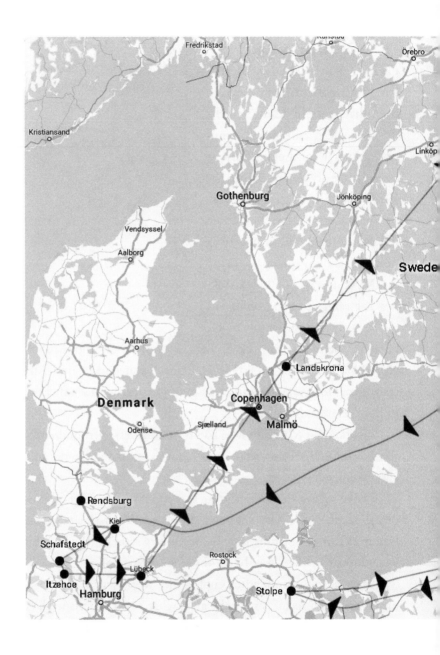

Route from the Libau ghetto through five concentration
camps to recovery centers and on to Stockholm.

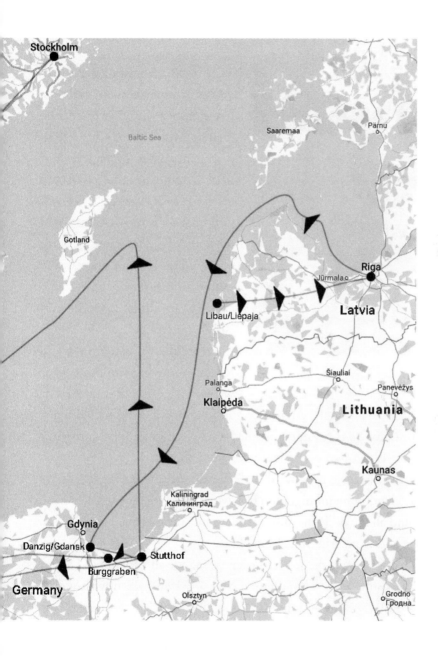

ly—just before the birth of the State of Israel—when the different Israe-li so-called "diplomats" at the time, came to our offices in Stockholm. It had such an impact on me.

Skiing in Sweden – March 1947

I recall the visit of Ben-Guri-on, his handshake and friendliness. I remember the visit of Moshe Sharett, who became the second prime minister of Israel; Berl Locker, who became chairman of the Jewish Agency;[45] Nahum Goldman, a leading Zionist and the founder and longtime president of the World Jewish Congress; and many other great Zionists who came to Stockholm to work fever-ishly in secret behind the scenes to secure the yes vote from world leaders going back to the League of Nations. There was no AIPAC (American Israel Public Affairs Committee) or other formal lobbying organizations. So it fell upon people—these leaders and the staff of the World Jewish Congress—to lobby for a Jewish homeland.

I remember the time we did all the secretive work for the *Aliyah Bet*, the clandestine immigration of Jews to Palestine between 1920 and 1948, and all the different missions that came up that made this such an exciting and wonderful time in my life.

I'll never forget the joy and excitement we all experienced at the World Jewish Congress building on May 14, 1948, when we heard on the radio David Ben-Gurion proclaiming the establishment of the State of Israel. He became the first premier of the State of Israel.

Our hearts were full and overflowing with joy. Yes, Jews across the

---

45   The Jewish Agency is charged with bringing Jews to Israel, Israel to Jews, and helping build a better society in Israel and beyond.

world felt that way, but to those of us who had endured the Holocaust experience, it was more than one can put into words. At least that's how it impacted me.

We waved the blue-and-white Israeli flag from the window of the World Jewish Congress building. Then we raced downstairs to dance in the street with fellow celebrants. Finally, the Jews of the world had somewhere to go! I was so happy to have the good fortune to witness the birth of the State of Israel. My Zionist dream came true. And Jenny and I were alive to witness this momentous day on behalf of our seventy-nine family members who had perished in the Holocaust.

I continued my efforts to acquire a visa to the United States, where my uncle Harry would sponsor Jenny and me. Uncle Ephraim Lovitt, whom we called Lester, also tried to expedite our documentation to allow us to enter the US.

In late 1946, the day finally arrived. Armed with my backup documentation, I eagerly waited in the hallway at the US embassy for my visa appointment. I was ushered into an office, where I sat across the desk from an embassy official. He looked through my documents and asked me several questions.

Then he announced, "The small quota for Latvians is closed."

"How long do I have to wait?" I asked.

Without hesitation, he casually said, "Oh, about ten years."

I was devastated. I would not be able to join our only remaining relatives—that we were aware of—in the United States.

I was ushered out of the office and slowly exited the embassy into the grayness outside and to a cloudy and uncertain future.

Fortunately, Roma had been born in Danzig before his parents moved to Libau. The Danzig visa requests for entry to the US had not yet surpassed the quota to the extent of Latvian requests, and he became eligible to enter the US. The wait would be approximately three years. That was the second-best news Roma had received that year. The best news was that Jenny had agreed to marry him!

On December 15, 1946, Roma and Jenny were married in the Great Synagogue of Stockholm with financial assistance from Hillel Storch, a generous couple by the name of Klein, and some funds from the king of Sweden, who kindly provided financial grants for refugees' life events. In Stockholm, Roma worked as an electrician, while Jenny worked as a seamstress in a wedding gown house.

Celebration before Roma and Jenny's wedding in Stockholm in 1946. Roma and Jenny standing fifth and sixth from right. Mrs. Klein standing extreme right. Fanny seated third from left

The happy but anxious couple were sponsored into the United States by Harry and Ruth Lowitz, based on the visa obtained by Roma under the Danzig allocation. Jenny and Roma arrived in New York from Sweden on April 11, 1949, and lived with my uncle and aunt in their apartment in the Bronx. It would be ten years before I would see them again.

Roma was hardworking, but opportunities were limited for immigrants, particularly those not fluent in English. He had a job carrying tar for road construction and worked as a delivery boy. This was humiliating for someone with the memory of a privileged childhood. Later he worked as an electrician, but like so many other immigrants, he was taken advantage of. Jenny took on seamstress projects to supplement the family's income and provide herself with a little spending money.

Roma and Jenny eventually moved into a rented apartment on Grand Concourse and had two daughters, Eileen and Sandy. Their apartment was on floor BB, the basement below the basement. Only the caretaker's small room, the incinerator, and the coal storage were on the same floor. The building's laundry room was one floor up on the first basement.

Roma Isakson

It was a small two-bedroom apartment, and they rented the second bedroom to another Jewish immigrant, Eddie Volkman, and his lovely Swedish wife who had converted to Judaism. Eddie was from Poland, and to the Jews of New York, Lithuania, Russia, and Latvia, "Polacks" were second-class citizens. But the kind, caring Isaksons treated them with respect and dignity, and the two couples became friends for life.

Meanwhile, I had given up on my efforts to obtain a US visa—which seemed stalled at every turn—and began working my connections in Stockholm to find work in Israel.

Eventually I was offered a nursing position at the hospital in Afula by Moshe Soroka, chief of Kupat Holim, the National Healthcare of Israel. I had met him when he visited the World Jewish Congress office. I told him it was my intention to move to Israel.

At the time, Afula had a population of twenty-three hundred Jews and ten Muslims. Twenty-two years earlier, the American Zionist Commonwealth completed a purchase of the Afula valley in northern Israel from the Sursuk family of Beirut. But Afula was a swamp with much disease and little transportation to the major Jewish areas of Israel.

"If you want to come to work in Israel, I will get you a job," he said. "But you would have to work in the swamps. After all you've gone through, do you still think you'd want to work there?"

"Yes," I responded enthusiastically.

CHAPTER TEN

A Change in Plans

Der Mensch Tracht, Un Gott Lacht
(Man plans, and God laughs).

—AN OLD YIDDISH ADAGE

A funny thing happened on the way to Afula…

One day, a lady walked into the World Jewish Congress office. I heard my name being called.

"Fanny?" the lady asked in an inquiring tone.

I turned around. She looked at me in astonishment.

"Etta," I replied, equally surprised.

"Fanny, I thought you were dead," she said.

"Etta, I thought you were dead, too," I responded.

Etta Segal and I had both grown up in Libau, and we had been detained together in the Libau ghetto. Etta had arrived in Stockholm from Poland, where she had been liberated by the Russians at a labor camp. Her father left for South Africa with her older brother before World War

II. Meanwhile, Etta, her mother, and another brother were captured by the Germans. Her mother and brother were exterminated by the Nazis.

Etta had married before the war, and she had lost her husband when the Germans occupied Libau. Etta Bojarsky, née Segal, had come to Stockholm to request a visa to be reunited with her father and older brother in South Africa.

There we stood, two young widows.

We were delighted and overwhelmed to see each other again. During that reunion, we didn't share our dreams or discuss our future. We just reminisced about our difficult past.

When I joined the Zionist organization Betar Youth Group in Libau as an eleven-year-old, my leader was a dashing young man named Louis Krashinsky. He left Libau in 1937 to avoid conscription into the Latvian army and joined his older brothers in South Africa. Bernard Kay and Julius Krasner, like many of the emigrants from eastern Europe, had anglicized their names. We corresponded occasionally.

Then the war came, and we lost touch.

Soon after landing in South Africa, my friend Etta attended a wedding with her father and brother. The bridegroom, Harry Hurwitz, was from Libau. He later became an advisor to Menachem Begin, who served as prime minister of Israel from 1977 to 1983.

Many of the guests at the wedding were from Libau. They asked Etta about various friends and relatives from Libau, wondering if they had survived the Holocaust. Unfortunately, none of them had survived the ravages of the Final Solution.

Then a young man recently arrived from Northern Rhodesia (now Zambia) approached Etta. He asked her about his family and members of the Betar group.

"I don't know about them," said Etta. "But you know who I saw in Sweden—Fanny Judelowitz."

Louis Krashinsky (now Krasner) couldn't believe it. He was speechless.

"Do you know where she is?" he asked.

She told him that I worked for the World Jewish Congress in Stockholm and gave Louis my contact information. The following day, I received a telegram from him telling me how happy he was to know that I was alive and safe. We started corresponding, informing each other about our respective experiences over the past several years.

After about a year, Louis asked, "Wouldn't you like to visit South Africa? You could do with a holiday."

I told him that I was going to Israel. That was my dream.

Jenny, for one, was very opposed to my plans to move to Israel.

"After all you've been through and the life you've had, you ought to go visit Louis in South Africa and not head to a swamp," said Jenny.

There was a lot going on in my life at that time. I had been so involved in the ongoing efforts for the establishment of the State of Israel, and I was meeting many influential people. But of course it was very special connecting with Louis again.

Frankly, I was perplexed. There were so many coincidences at work here. The fact I happened to be in Stockholm, the fact that Etta walked into the World Jewish Congress offices, the fact that she was headed to Johannesburg, and the fact that Etta, her father, and brother were invited to the same wedding that Louis would be attending. Clearly, the stars were all aligning.

And Jenny kept the pressure on.

"You've endured so much already in your life," she said. "You deserve a little bit of peace. And you know him. Go visit him."

In addition to his many letters, Louis called me on the phone several times, which was unheard of in those days. After more than a year of correspondence with Louis—and with strong encouragement from Jenny, who now had a visa with her husband, Roma, to enter the US—I agreed to visit Johannesburg in November 1948 on my way to live in Afula, Israel.

Getting from Stockholm to Johannesburg was challenging, to say the least. There were no direct flights. I vividly remember the exhausting and circuitous journey.

The first stop was Brussels, where I took the opportunity to attend the opera, my passion. From Brussels, I traveled to Amsterdam, where I boarded KLM Dutch Airlines for the flight to Johannesburg.

The first refueling stop was in the northern region of Cameroon. As I stepped off the plane to stretch my legs, I experienced culture shock. There were flies, flies, flies, and more flies, everywhere. And all I could see were extremely tall local African men, each wearing a red fez with a tassel, making them appear even more enormous. This was such a sharp contrast from Stockholm. I was really intimidated.

On the flight, I sat beside a really nice British man. He was an architect heading to an assignment to build a bridge in Southern Rhodesia (now Zimbabwe). When we settled in for the next leg of the trip, I started sobbing. This was Africa. I figured I would be living in the huts we saw outside the airport among intimidating giants. Afula started looking a whole lot better!

The architect tried to calm me down. He assured me that Johannesburg was nothing like this. He said it was a real city, very European-like.

Then we landed in Nairobi, Kenya, for our next refueling stop. As I peered out the window and viewed the surroundings, determined not to leave the plane, I began to question the architect's description of Johannesburg.

I stepped off the plane at the Palmietfontein International Airport in Johannesburg to find Louis; his sister-in-law, Jean Kay; and his black assistant, Steve, waiting on the tarmac to meet me. Steve was there to take my luggage to Louis's small black Ford convertible in the parking lot.

I reached out to shake Louis's and Jean's hands. Jean looked on disapprovingly as I also shook Steve's hand. Later, I asked Louis about Jean's reaction at the airport.

"White women don't touch black men in South Africa," Louis explained.

I burst into tears. I had just lived through discrimination and persecution at its worst, and now this!

In 1948, the National Party gained power in South Africa, and its all-white government began enforcing existing racial segregation and white supremacy policies instituted shortly after South Africa gained independence from Great Britain in 1910. Later these laws added additional race classifications—colored (mixed race) and Asian (Indian and Pakistani)—and also separated Bantu (blacks) from each other, dividing black South Africans along tribal lines in order to decrease their political power. This policy was called Apartheid (apartness or separate development). Apartheid laws limited contact between white and nonwhite South Africans, who were forced to live in separate geographic areas and use separate public facilities, and banned marriages between whites and people of other races, prohibited sexual relations between black and white South Africans, and reserved specific jobs for different races. These laws sanctioning racial segregation and political and economic discrimination against nonwhites remained in place until 1991.

I really didn't know what to expect from Johannesburg, or from Louis for that matter. After he left Libau in 1937, he occasionally wrote to his Betar group to find out how we were doing. I had always liked him and had learned so much from him. He had many talents—he had a wonderful singing voice, he was a great athlete, and he was highly intelligent. And he was very charismatic.

I had last seen Louis when I was fifteen years old. And, now here I was at twenty-six being in his presence once again. Of course, after everything I had experienced during those years, I felt like I was eighty-six.

I received such a warm and wonderful welcome from him. It was as if we had known each other all our lives. It was a wonderful reunion. He was everything I remembered him to be—and more. The mutual attraction was so natural. It rekindled memories from when I was a young girl and we had a certain chemistry.

After three weeks, we were engaged. And on January 2, 1949—six weeks after arriving in Johannesburg—I married the charming ex-Rhodesian from Libau, Madrich Louis Krasner, who was now a resident of Johannesburg.

Louis bought me a wedding dress from an exclusive boutique owned by Minna Brenner, who was also originally from Libau. We were married at the Sydenham Highlands North Synagogue with a wedding reception at the Hebrew Order of David (HOD) hall. It was an emotional day with lots of tears and celebration.

For me, however, my wedding day was bittersweet. I adored Louis, but I felt very alone. I didn't have any family members with me. Jenny was still in Stockholm and couldn't afford to fly to Johannesburg. I hadn't known any of the guests at my wedding more than a few weeks. Louis had a lot of friends and family. He had two brothers living there.

My most gratifying memory of the wedding was witnessing Louis's pure joy and elation. He was surrounded by his brothers

Louis and Fanny's wedding photo

and many friends from his sports activities and an active Jewish communal life.

We began our family almost immediately. Our first son, Harold, was born November 25, 1949. It was probably the happiest day of my life. Later, we had a daughter, Shirley, born October 23, 1951, and a second son, Milton, born April 14, 1956. I considered it a miracle that I was able to have children. Many of the women who survived the camps were unable to conceive due to their poor living conditions and diet. For me, producing a family was and is a gift from a higher being.

On honeymoon at Riviera Hotel near Johannesburg – January 1949

Louis Krasner's introduction to southern Africa was not all smooth sailing. He arrived in South Africa in 1937 with ten dollars in his pocket and was met by his two brothers, who had left Latvia a few years earlier. His brother Julius Krasner worked at Weinberg Jewelry Factory in Johannesburg, where he was able to find a job for Louis.

Louis had excellent experience in jewelry design, engraving, and manufacturing. After attending the gymnasium in Libau, he had been trained and apprenticed by a German meister jeweler.

Unfortunately, South African prime minister General Jan Smuts and his government had instituted strict visa restrictions on immigrants from Europe and enforced the Quota Act of 1930, which was intended to curtail the entry of Jews into South Africa. After six months, Louis was forced to leave his job and the country.

He traveled to a relatively new town in Northern Rhodesia called Kitwe. Kitwe was founded in 1936 in north-central Zambia as the railway that was completed in 1937 was being built by explorer Cecil

John Rhodes's company. The expanding copper mines at nearby Nkana increased Kitwe's significance over the years, and it finally became the second-largest city in Zambia decades later.

Living in a dilapidated storeroom with no utilities and only a cot to sleep on, Louis worked for a liquor store delivering spirits to colonialists for their daily afternoon sundowners. These were difficult times, and Louis applied for a job at the nearby Nkana copper mines.

While standing in line, he struck up a conversation with another job seeker about soccer, or football, as it is usually called. He mentioned that while in Latvia he had played against a well-known Viennese team called Hakoah. The other gentleman was so impressed he invited Louis to try out for the local soccer team. Louis was a natural sportsman and became a star on the team. Louis eventually played on the national soccer team for Northern Rhodesia in 1941. He never did get a job in the mines.

Northern Rhodesia National Soccer team. Louis in front row left with ball

The soccer team traveled to play in Élisabethville (now called Lubumbashi) in the southeastern part of the Belgian Congo (now the Democratic Republic of the Congo). After the match, Louis asked a teammate to walk with him through the village to get the flavor of this African town. Louis saw a jewelry store, crossed the road, and peered in the window.

He pointed to a ring on display and said to his friend, "I made that ring." His friend chided him, thinking he was joking.

Krashinsky family circa 1926 (back row, left to right): Irving, Julius, Joe, Bernard, father Mones. (front row, left to right): mother Leah, Rosa, Louis

They entered the store and Louis asked the owner if the ring came from Weinberg's in Johannesburg. The owner confirmed Louis's observation, and they spent time discussing the jewelry business. The owner was so impressed by Louis's knowledge of jewelry that they reached a partnership arrangement for a new store—Star Jewelers—in Kitwe.

Louis ran the store for eight years until he received permission to reenter South Africa, where he attended his friends' (Harry and Frieda Hurwitz) wedding. And that's where he found me through his conversation with Etta. That fortuitous meeting worked out pretty well for me. Israel would have to wait. Funny how life works. Another miracle, you might say.

CHAPTER ELEVEN

Embracing Life in Johannesburg

I'm just trying to get back to normal life.

—CHRIS KYLE, A UNITED STATES NAVY SEAL
VETERAN AND SNIPER WHO SERVED FOUR TOURS
IN THE IRAQ WAR

Louis and I enjoyed a full and active life in South Africa. We raised our three children, and together we built and ran a successful jewelry business—Star Jewelers—first in Mayfair, Johannesburg, and then downtown at the corner of Von Brandis and Bree Streets in the Jewish Guild Building.

Meanwhile, we became deeply involved in the Jewish community and local organizations in Johannesburg. Among others, we were associated with the Jewish Guild sports and social club, the Maccabiah Organization, the Revisionist Party, the Houghton Golf and Lawn Bowling

Club, the Hebrew School PTA Board, and the Women's Israel Zionist Organization (WIZO).

Louis's first jewelry store in Mayfair, a suburb of Johannesburg

We were active supporters of Tel Hai Fund, an organization in Israel for orphans and troubled children who had lost their way. In fact, Louis served as vice chairman of the fund for many years. We devoted financial resources and even held an annual lawn bowling tournament at the Jewish Guild as a fundraiser for Tel Hai. The children's center was located where the Battle of Tel Hai was fought on March 1, 1920, between Shiite Arab militia who, accompanied by Bedouin from a nearby village, attacked the Jewish agricultural village of Tel Hai in northern Galilee. In the battle, Joseph Trumpeldor, the commander of Jewish defenders of Tel Hai, and for whom Betar was named, was killed. Some scholars saw this outbreak of violence as a prelude to the Arab-Israeli conflict three decades later.

Louis was known as one of the "three Louis"—Louis Krasner, Louis Gecelter, and Louis Kriel—the founders who acquired the grounds for the building of the Jewish Guild country club and sports facility at a time when Jews were not welcome at the premier country clubs of Johannesburg.

There is a long and influential history of Jews in South Africa, starting with Portuguese Jewish cartographers and scientists who contributed to Vasco da Gama's discovery of the Cape of Good Hope in 1497. Despite restrictions against the immigration of non-Christians, there were a number of nonprofessing Jews among the first settlers of Cape Town in 1652 and then again in the early 1800s as part of the Dutch East India Company, which required all employees and colonists to be Protestant.

Religious freedom was granted by the Dutch colony in 1803 and guaranteed by the British in 1806. Jewish immigrants from Germany and Holland arrived in Cape Town in the early nineteenth century seeking fortune and adventure. As the Dutch Boers moved inland away from the British, Jews established trading stores in villages and at railway stations, which soon became local business centers for the Boer farmers. They established a credit system to finance new industries and were active in the production of wine, clothing, and steel. By midcentury Jews developed shipping, fishing, and coastal trading and sugar enterprises. The first South African synagogue, Tikvat Israel (Hope of Israel, referring to the Cape of Good Hope) was established in 1849 and is still an active congregation in Cape Town. While the original building no longer exists, its two historical replacements remain in the Cape Town Botanical Gardens, along with the South African Jewish Museum.

The discovery of diamonds in 1867 in Kimberley attracted Jewish entrepreneurs and businessmen from all over the world, including Barney Barnato and Sammy Marks. Barnato founded the De Beers Consolidated Mines for mining the Kimberley diamond fields, and Marks, after working at menial jobs on arrival, became an agricultural, industrial, and mining tycoon, developing the Witwatersrand gold fields, coal mines, fruit farms, forests, bricks, glass, steel, and leather goods manufacturing, and established South African

Breweries. Marks openly practiced Judaism and served as a mediator between the British and the Boers during the second Boer-British Wars of 1899–1902, eventually serving in the first South African Parliament in 1910.

Between 1880 and 1910, the Jewish population swelled to around forty thousand, with immigrants arriving mainly from Lithuania fleeing political persecution and pogroms in Europe. These immigrants adopted Anglo-Jewish customs and infused a strong Zionist connection.

In 1903, attempts were made to restrict immigration. But a strong Jewish lobby influenced legislation, and between 1920 and 1930, some twenty thousand Jewish immigrants from eastern Europe arrived in South Africa. In 1930, increased feelings of anti-Semitism and the rise of Nazism in Germany sparked the passing of the Quota Act, restricting immigration from Greece, Latvia, Lithuania, Poland, Russia, and Palestine, but not Germany. While not expressly stated, the aim of the Quota Act was to restrict Jewish immigration. The German loophole was closed with the passing of the Aliens Act in 1937 as Nazism influenced militant and nationalistic Afrikaners and anti-Semitic organizations emerged. Further concerns and fear arose when the anti-Jewish National Party came to power in 1948. Throughout the twentieth century, there were divisions among the whites. Although not formal, whites were regarded as either English (of British descent), Afrikaans (of Dutch descent), or Jewish (more than 85 percent being from Lithuania). Anti-Semitism was subtler among some, but it was pervasive.

While most Jews stayed away from politics, focusing on family and economic matters, many were actively involved in the anti-Apartheid movement and some were co-defendants with Nelson Mandela at trials for treason in 1956 and anti-Apartheid activities in 1963. Mandela later wrote, "I have found Jews to be more broadminded than most whites on issues of race and politics, perhaps because they themselves have historically been victims of prejudice." Mandela's defense attorney in the 1956 trial in which he prevailed was renowned jurist Issie Maisels, who was a committed and practicing Jew.

Jews were disproportionately represented in the commercial and financial sectors of society. The Jewish population peaked in the early 1970s, reaching nearly 120,000, mainly concentrated in Johannesburg and Cape Town.

Between 1970 and 1992, about forty thousand Jews left South Africa. During this same period, approximately ten thousand Israelis moved into the country.

Sports played a major role in our family. Louis was a wonderful tennis player, but our preferred sport was lawn bowls. Our sons, Harold and Milton, excelled at tennis, golf, and cricket, and our daughter, Shirley, was a fine dancer and ballerina.

In addition, I served as president of the Jewish Guild Bowls activities. In 1962, the World Lawn Bowls Championships were held in Seattle. Louis had the honor of being selected to represent South Africa, and our nation went on to win the tournament to become world champions. It was very exciting.

(left to right): Harold, Louis, Shirley, Fanny and Milton at Jan Smuts Airport in Johannesburg in 1962 as Louis leaves for World Bowls Championship in Seattle

Later, we joined Houghton Golf and Bowls Country Club, an upscale club near our home in the center of an affluent suburb of Johannesburg. I held the post of president of the ladies' section for four years. I also won the Houghton women's singles championship in bowls. Louis won many competitions and medals, going back to 1932 in Libau. A certificate of his sporting achievements was deposited in the Maccabi village museum during our trip to Israel in 1978. As a family, we were a bunch of very competitive individuals, always driven to excel and to win. And we always rooted for each other.

President of the Houghton Golf and   Louis with his trophy from the World
Bowls Country Club   Bowls Championship in Seattle in 1962

Louis and I did our best to create a loving, happy home life with our children, Harold, Shirley, and Milton. Louis was a community leader with a strong, charismatic personality belying his small physical stature. With me by his side, he was usually the center of attention at social occasions. He also had a keen sense of humor. As the kids often said, he would tell a joke and laugh before delivering the punch line.

"We had a wonderful family life," said Shirley. "My parents always did things together. My mother was very supportive of my father. She never contradicted him. She always used to say, 'We support each other whatever our decisions are, even though we might not agree with each other.'"

Fanny in Johanneburg—1962

(left to right): Shirley, Fanny, Louis and Harold at beach in Durban – July 1955

Our family always had meals together. We entertained a lot, and it was not uncommon for us to have large gatherings for dinner. Louis had a large family with many nieces and nephews. And we had made a lot of friends through the children's schools.

On Friday nights, we often invited relatives and friends over for Shabbat dinner. Shirley fondly remembers her assignment.

"When I was young, my job was to set the table," she said. "My mother would set one place and show me how to do it. Then I would set the rest of the place settings. We would often have thirty-five people for dinner."

Our dinner guests often included my closest friend, Essie; her husband, Jimmy; and their son, Malcolm.

I reconnected with Essie on a visit to the post office in Johannesburg in 1949 while I was pregnant with Harold. We were so thrilled to see each other.

"Essie, you're alive," I shouted.

Essie was from Libau and had lived in the ghetto with me during the war. She had been married, but her husband had been killed along with the other men during the July 1941 *Aktion* in Libau.

When Essie was liberated, she married a man named Jimmy Thwaites, whom she met in a displaced persons camp. He was a Scottish soldier who was a guard at the camp. They fell in love and got married. After Jimmy was discharged from the military, they moved to Scotland, where they lived with Jimmy's mother. Later, they had a baby named Malcolm and moved to South Africa, where Essie's sister lived.

After our reunion at the post office, Essie and I made arrangements to meet again with our spouses. We became very close friends. In fact, it was Louis who arranged with the chief rabbi of Johannesburg, Rabbi Rabinowitz, for Malcolm to be circumcised at age eight with the blessing of his father and Jewish mother.

Although we were both Holocaust survivors, Essie and I didn't talk about our experiences in front of others. We occasionally spoke about it in private.

As Essie and her family were often at our home for Shabbat dinner, our children became close with Malcolm.

Attendance at Shabbat dinner was mandatory for family members.

"I never missed a Friday night dinner at home," said Harold. "If I wanted to see my girlfriend, it would have to be before or after Friday night dinner."

With Louis and me working together at the store, some sacrifices had to be made, as the children understood.

"Growing up, we never took vacations together as a family unit," recalled Milton. "My father felt he couldn't get away from the store. I think he only made it to two of my soccer games."

Occasionally, I would take the three children on vacation with me, usually to the beach in Durban. Once Harold became involved in the business, it took some of the pressure off and gave Louis and me the freedom to travel. We were able to take a trip overseas together.

"From about the age of sixteen, I would begin to help them out in the store after school and during college," said Harold, who received a degree in economics from the University of the Witwatersrand. "In 1972, I went overseas for nine months to Switzerland (Lucerne) and England (London) to take a management course in the jewelry industry and learn all I could about the business."

I wanted a normal life for my family and never shared my pain or complained. This was a mother's love, a gift to my children. In fact, when Harold was fifteen years old and unaware of my history, he was helping his father clean out his study and came across a book of photos of the Holocaust. He remembers asking Louis if the Holocaust really happened. His father confirmed the historical accuracy but made no mention of my experiences or involvement.

"I sensed my mother was holding something back," said Shirley. "I knew she was in the Holocaust, but she rarely spoke about it. Holocaust Memorial Day at West Park Cemetery was such an important day for her. She made sure we were all there. The events were painted with a broad brush. She never went into individual stories."

Discussions of our childhood experiences in Libau rarely surfaced in our home in Johannesburg.

"Every once in a while, my parents touched on their childhood in Latvia," said Milton. "But it was a total disconnect for me. They used to talk in Yiddish. They didn't teach us Yiddish because they didn't want us to find out what they were talking about."

It was through Malcolm Thwaites that Shirley would meet her husband, Howard First. Malcolm and Howard lived in the same suburb of Johannesburg. They were friends through school and then were classmates in dental school. Of course Malcolm knew Harold, Milton, and Shirley from our Friday night dinners.

Malcolm set up a date between Howard and Shirley. I remember the evening Howard came by to pick up Shirley. He rang the doorbell, and I opened the door. In front of me stood a very nice young man. I looked him over from head to toe. As my eyes shifted downward, I noticed he was wearing moccasins on his feet. Of course I didn't make any negative remarks at the time. Then Shirley arrived at the door and off they went.

When Shirley returned home that night, I asked her, "What kind of man shows up to take out a young lady on a date wearing moccasins?"

When Shirley relayed the story to Howard, he doubled over laughing. And naturally it has become a running joke. Over the years, Howard has teased me incessantly because I didn't approve of his moccasins. Whenever he has the opportunity, he'll say, "I'm the man with the moccasins."

Weekends were family time, often spent at the Jewish Guild, where Louis and I played bowls while the children swam and played tennis. Harold fondly recalls those hectic Sundays in Johannesburg.

"My father and some of the choir, including me on occasion, would sing at weddings and then rush over to the bowling green for my father's afternoon match," he said.

But not even Louis's beloved bowling could supersede his love for singing. And nothing was more important to Louis than Zionism and Israel.

It was Louis who brought Yiddishkeit (the Jewish way of life), its customs and practices into our home. He was learned in Jewish texts, enjoyed davening and leading prayers in synagogue, and loved singing, particularly Jewish music and cantorial chants. Louis read and scored music and for twenty-one years served as choirmaster at the large Sydenham-Highlands North Synagogue in Johannesburg. Meanwhile, I was never far away, sitting upstairs in the synagogue opposite the choir adjudicating my husband's performance.

Just like in my childhood home, music was an integral part of the Krasner family home. Every Friday night after Shabbat dinner, the family and our guests would retire to the living room for group sing-alongs, with Harold or Shirley playing the piano. Louis, who had extensive musical training, possessed a fantastic tenor voice. Milton also sang and played the flute beautifully.

Family photo at Harold's Bar Mitzvah – 1962

Music has been a lifelong passion of mine and has provided wonderful memories. From my youth in Libau when I listened to my mother playing piano or attended opera with my parents, to the Libau ghetto "concerts" in which I occasionally participated by singing in several languages, to the awful German songs I was forced to sing by the SS while marching to work, to attending opera in Stockholm, to attending a philharmonic concert with Louis on my second day in Africa and every other chance I had, music has been a cherished interest of mine. I used to take Milton to the symphony at the Johannesburg City Hall and get seats at the back of the stage so we could be close to the orchestra and be able to follow the conductor.

While my taste in music is eclectic, opera and classical are my favorites. I'll never forget the thrill I experienced attending the concerts of great violinists like Yehudi Menuhin and Isaac Stern. But the greatest enjoyment came from magical music nights at home or listening to the synagogue choir with Louis and the children in Johannesburg.

When our first grandchild, Kim, was born in 1974, it was an indescribable feeling of joy for me and Louis. That was because my children never had the opportunity to meet a single grandparent. And our parents never lived to experience a single moment of joy from their grandchildren.

So you can imagine how special it was for us to have the good fortune to become grandparents in our lifetime. Then along came Lauri and all the others after that. Kim and Lauri were born in South Africa, while the others were born in the United States.

Louis and I rarely had disagreements, but whenever we went out, he always wondered why it took me so long to get ready. That was his pet peeve!

"That was the major battle in our home—waiting for my mother to get ready," said Milton. "My mother would take too long to get ready as far as my father was concerned. Now she calls me if I'm running late and says, 'How come you're not here?'"

It was Louis, the Jabotinsky Zionist and Menachem Begin supporter, who instilled a deep love for Israel in our children.

Louis's close friend Harry Hurwitz, the editor of the *Jewish Heritage* newspaper in Johannesburg, moved to Jerusalem and became an advisor to Menachem Begin when the latter became prime minister of Israel in 1977. Hurwitz then served as information attaché at the Israeli Embassy in Washington under Ambassador Moshe Arens during the years in which Israel bombed Iraq's nuclear reactor in Osirak (1981) and invaded Lebanon (1982). He was responsible for building the Menachem Begin Heritage Center in Jerusalem. Through Harry, our family and the Begins became friendly. One of my most treasured mementos is an invitation to the *bat mitzvah* of Hasya Begin, their eldest daughter, in April 1958.

My love and devotion to Israel can be traced back to my childhood. But my first trip to Israel in 1958 to participate in the tenth anniversary celebration of the State of Israel really cemented those feelings. Landing in Israel, feeling the Holy Land under my feet, feeling at home in a country I had never seen but always imagined was simply overwhelming.

As tears rolled down my cheeks, I recalled the many meetings and youth camps in Latvia where as children and teenagers, we sang and danced and expressed our yearning for Eretz Yisrael—the Land of Israel, a homeland for the Jewish people. It was a dream then, and now I was living my dream.

Hebrew songs with lyrics such as "From the heights of Mount Scopus I greet thee, O Jerusalem, through all ages I have dreamt to behold thee" and "The hope of an Israel on both sides of the Jordan, this is ours, this too" jumped to my mind on the tarmac at Ben-Gurion airport.

It also took me back to those days when we worked feverishly behind the scenes at the World Jewish Congress in Sweden for a yes vote in favor of the establishment of a state for the Jewish people.

I'll never forget the sheer elation we felt on May 14, 1948, when my dream came true and the State of Israel was born. How fortunate I was to be one of the very few members of my Betar group and family to have the privilege to return "home."

My visit to Israel in 1958 was made even more special by a reunion with my second cousin Iska Funkelshtein, who had changed his name to Leshem after the war. Iska lived in Aizpute, and our families would spend part of the summers together. We became great friends. He moved away to work in Riga. After the Germans invaded, he was incarcerated in the Riga ghetto and then sent to Kaiserwald concentration camp. He escaped from Kaiserwald and traveled east, where he joined the Russian army.

After the war, he escaped Russia and joined his sister in Kibbutz Kfar Blum in northern Israel. Iska found me through the Red Cross and contacted me when I was in Sweden. It would be ten years before we would see each other again, at an emotional reunion in Ashkelon, a development started by South Africans. During my five weeks in Israel, Iska escorted me everywhere. From the Ramat Gan Stadium for the tenth-anniversary celebrations of the State of Israel to his kibbutz with the huge statue of Mordechai Anielewicz, who led the Jewish Fighting Organization in the Warsaw Ghetto Uprising, the largest Jewish insurrection during World War II.

(left to right): Cousins Zali Isakovitz, Fanny, Iska Funkelstein-late spring 1940

Iska is a hero to me. Upon arrival in Israel, he joined the Israeli army and fought in every conflict from 1948 to the mid-1980s before retiring as a major from the Israel Defense Forces (IDF). He gave his entire life to the security, defense, and well-being of our homeland. I saw him on every visit I made to Israel, including at the Protea Retirement Home, also started by South African Jews, shortly before his passing. He left an indelible impact on me of bravery and commitment to ensuring "never again."

On that journey to Israel in 1958, I made a couple of stops for business in Italy and France to review the latest jewelry fashions and purchase product for the store in Johannesburg before heading to New York to see my sister Jenny for the first time in ten years.

Jenny and Roma had immigrated to the US in early 1949. After my visit to New York, I traveled to Las Vegas, San Diego, and San Francisco before flying home to Johannesburg. It was rare for women to fly around the world by themselves in those days, but I found it interesting, invigorating, and exciting.

On my stop in Paris, I visited with Louis's cousin Judith Polonski (née Goodman), who had married the son of our rabbi from Libau, Rabbi Isser Polonski. His son had moved to Paris and was an architect and rumored to be an ardent communist.

I spent a marvelous day with Judith and her family. She was fun and really smart. She had left Libau to study science at the Sorbonne University in Paris. Judith had won the Madame Curie Medal for Science for her work as one of the rare female directors of research at the Centre nationale de la recherche scientifique (CNRS). I believe she received a small Citroën convertible as one of her prizes or used her prize money to purchase the car.

On Bastille Day—July 14, 1958—we traveled up and down the Champs-Élysées in her Citroën from the Place de la Concorde to the Arc de Triomphe and back again. All the while, I stood on the passenger seat, waving and laughing as we passed all the theaters, cafés, and luxury shops. What an experience!

But some memories were still raw. After we parted, I began thinking about her father-in-law, the wonderful Rabbi Polonski. He was a very pleasant, attractive, and learned man with a thick black beard. He was a teacher, accountant, and rabbi. He was truly beloved by his congregants and the greater Libau Jewish community.

In mid-July 1941, the Nazis, as part of their determination to humiliate and torment the Jews, found several bearded Jews and dragged them into Rabbi Polonski's Choral Synagogue.

Then, as described in Kalman Linkimer's diary,[46] "There, the Nazis ordered them to put on prayer shawls, handed each of them two Torah scrolls, and with various kinds of mockery ordered them to walk back to the Firehouse Square."

Linkimer describes how the Nazis unrolled the Torah scrolls and ordered the Jews to walk on the scrolls and shout, "Our God has died, long live our God Hitler."

Each one resisted, and they were savagely beaten. After the Jews collapsed, the Nazis dragged them by their hands and feet over the Torah scrolls.

Then it was Rabbi Polonski's turn. He didn't resist but walked defiantly alongside the Torah scrolls without defiling them. He weathered the threats and blows for avoiding trampling the scrolls until he collapsed unconscious from the beatings that rained down on him. He was thrown into prison and shot later that day at the naval base with many other Jews.

And that is how life is for us survivors. Even happy events, if in some tangential way connected to the Holocaust, continue to generate painful memories. No wonder so many of us chose not to discuss our experiences for so long. It's a matter of self-protection and preservation, maybe even sanity.

---

46   *19 Months in a Cellar: How 11 Jews Eluded Hitler's Henchmen: The Holocaust Diary of Kalman Linkimer 1941–1945*, ed. Edward Anders, trans. by Rebecca Margolis, p. 12.

CHAPTER TWELVE

Land of the Free

*What made America great was her
ability to transform her own dream
into hope for all mankind.*

—NICOLAS SARKOZY

At the annual Jewish Federation of San Diego County Men's Event in December 2012, my grandson Ari Krasner began the proceedings with a stirring rendition of "The Star-Spangled Banner" before a crowd of nearly one thousand attendees at the Del Mar Fairgrounds. I wondered how he could possibly grasp the symbolism of his own family's journey as he belted out, "o'er the land of the free and the home of the brave." Ari had grown up free, and yet he had a deep appreciation for the bravery of his grandparents in eastern Europe and in southern Africa.

My immediate family's pilgrimage to the United States began in 1977. Our youngest son, Milton, moved to the US to attend Fairleigh Dickinson University in Teaneck, New Jersey. Not yet twenty-one, Milton was eligible to receive his visa as a minor family member. He then transferred to Montclair State, where he played on the soccer team.

During the first year, he lived with Aunt Jenny and Uncle Roma. As Milton became better acquainted with his aunt and uncle, he was astounded to hear Roma's stories about me and what Roma referred to as "your mother's courageous acts" during the war.

"Uncle Roma always used to talk about how my mother saved Jenny during the war," said Milton. "But he used to do it in a joking way. I never knew how serious he was. Aunt Jenny didn't mention anything, but Roma started telling me all these crazy stories about the Holocaust. I was immature at the time. He would give me information in bits and pieces. It was totally disjointed. He would carry on as if I should have known what he was talking about, but I had no idea.

"I was surprised to learn how close Roma had come to being shot. As an electrician, he used to short out the power at the camps. Then he would have a certain amount of time to get as much food—potato skins and that sort of thing—as possible. He was within seconds of getting caught. If he were caught, he would've been shot on sight. That was really powerful to me."

This information was a revelation to Milton because I had never discussed my experiences during the war in front of the children in our home. Louis had lost his family, and it didn't seem appropriate for me to talk about my past. The one time I shared a little bit of information about my war experience with the children was during a Holocaust memorial ceremony in Johannesburg in the early 1970s.

Over the years, Roma proved to be strong and forceful, not to mention detail oriented and quick tempered. He also displayed deep affection for me and my family. He was quite concerned when our oldest son, Harold, entered the South African army for compulsory military training after high school in 1967, followed by three weeks of military camps per year for the next five years.

Roma and Jenny, through tapes we exchanged by mail, implored Louis and me to immigrate and not take the risk of sacrificing our son for the cause of an Apartheid system. Then, in May 1976, Roma asked Louis to meet with an immigration lawyer—a Mr. Blecher from Philadelphia—who was visiting Johannesburg.

By November 1976, Harold was arranging his American permanent residence green card as a diamond specialist in a diamond-cutting business. This was the result of a sponsorship by a gemologist and a fellow Holocaust survivor, Eddie Volkman, the close friend of Roma's who shared the apartment with the Isaksons way back in the "basement below the basement" on Grand Concourse.

But first, Harold and his new bride, Joy, had to get health clearance and needed chest x-rays. Harold remembers well the trip to the medical offices in the Lister Building in Johannesburg.

"Joy and I parked outside the building, and like a gentleman with a beautiful new wife, I walked around the car and opened her door," said Harold.

"I'm not going," replied Joy.

What Joy meant was that she was not going to the United States and thus not going for x-rays. Her father had recently passed away, and Joy did not feel comfortable leaving her mother behind in South Africa.

But they had put so much time and effort into planning and organizing their immigration. And Roma viewed Harold and Joy's immigration as a gateway to Louis and me entering the US.

In a moment of desperation, Harold claims—and Joy disputes—that he physically lifted Joy out of the car against her will and carried her upstairs to have the x-rays taken. In April 1978, they immigrated to San Diego.

Our daughter, Shirley, and her husband, Howard First, a dentist, immigrated in August 1978 under a visa through Howard's brother, Roy, who was already in the United States. Howard and Shirley settled for two years in Los Angeles, where Howard was an associate professor at the UCLA dental school. Although Shirley had a Bachelor of Arts degree and a teaching diploma, she never taught in the United States.

One thing you never fully appreciate or understand is the impact you have on others. Sometimes you just need to be reminded. While on a visit to New Jersey to see Jenny and Roma one year, I met a woman who began sobbing after being introduced to me. She held my hand and thanked me profusely.

Then she began to relate the story of her husband, Hershey Dorbian, who had recently passed away. She said that Hershey would often talk about me and how he wished he could meet me again and thank me for saving his life.

A twelve-year-old boy from Libau, Hershey had come into the emergency room at the Stolp labor camp in 1944. He was suffering from a very high fever that lasted several days. The commandant kept close tabs on him, as they needed his bed for new patients and Hershey's health was not improving.

The clock was ticking, and it was time for Hershey to leave, which I knew meant that he would disappear like the rest of the "too sick to work" prisoners. I reacted instinctively. I interceded and convinced the commandant that Hershey would be ready for work the next day. I did all that I could over the next twenty or so hours to get Hershey out of his bed by the time the commandant did his next day's rounds. From then on, I took Hershey under my wing. His mother and two sisters were part of a different Kazernierung, and aside from his cousin, whose job was to clean the boots and do other menial jobs for the Gestapo murderers, he had no one.

Hershey never forgot what I had done to save his life. And his widow made sure to let me know.

There were other young boys, like a twelve-year-old from Poland whose last name was Lieber. They had absolutely nobody to care for them. I played the role of mother/caregiver when I could. Another was George Schwab, who after the war became a professor of history at the City College of the City University of New York (CUNY) and started the Latvian Society and periodic newsletter. He later visited me at my home in Johannesburg.

After the ghetto, George had been separated from his mother. His father, Aron, a prominent physician in Libau died an especially gruesome death on July 29, 1941. "They gouged out one of his eyes and tortured him until he himself begged to be killed," according to Max Kaufman's book about the Latvian ghettos.[47] George's brother, Bernhard (Boris), who was my classmate at the gymnasium, was killed exactly three years later after a selection in Riga.

With our children safely ensconced in the US, Louis and I decided to move stateside in 1979. We received green cards through Jenny under privileges granted to siblings.

We had planned to move to America for several years, but to uproot from South Africa after having lived there for the longest stretch—thirty-one years—of my life was difficult. Nevertheless, the lure to be near family was too strong.

I was so grateful to immigrate to America. I thoroughly embraced all the tenets of freedom—life, liberty, and the pursuit of happiness. After enduring Apartheid in South Africa, it was so energizing to arrive in America, land of the free.

---

47   Max Kaufman, foreword to Churbn Lettland: *The Destruction of the Jews of Latvia*, trans. Foreword by George Schwab. Translated from German by Laimdota Mazzarins. Edited by Gertrude Schneider and Erhard Roy Wiehn. Hartung-Gorre Publishers: Konstanz, Germany. 2010

We relocated to San Diego to be with our growing family, including Louis's brothers, Irving and Julius Krasner.

At age sixteen, Irving was employed as a potato peeler on a ship. The ship left Libau headed for New York. Upon arrival in New York, the ship's workers were allowed to disembark for a few hours of land leave. Irving never returned to the ship.

He sought out a distant Hirschhorn cousin, with whom he stayed for a while. But he couldn't remain in the US without immigration papers, so he went to Tijuana, Mexico. From Tijuana, he eventually moved across the border to San Diego, where he started a business—Star Jewelers. His brother Julius followed him to San Diego.

There was so much to look forward to in retirement. Travel, sports, community, and family. A new and exciting future in America awaited us.

Nine months after moving to San Diego, Louis and I planned a road trip to include lawn bowls tournaments in Southern and Northern California and Nevada. We were both passionate about bowls and had won numerous club championships between us. Louis was a world-champion bowler and had been chosen to represent the US in the Maccabi Games in Israel.

Our vacation started wonderfully when Louis won the Walt Disney Lawn Bowling men's singles title in Beverly Hills, an auspicious beginning to his US campaign. Our next stop was San Francisco, where Louis did extremely well in the bowls tournament there. There, we met up with our niece, Sandy (Jenny and Roma's daughter), and her husband, Michael Monteko, for a few days. Louis and Michael conducted some investment business.

Then it was on the road again to Reno for another successful bowls tournament, followed by a little gambling at the casino, another pastime enjoyed by Louis. Louis spent the evening playing blackjack while I enjoyed keno. We were enjoying life.

After midnight, Louis suggested we get some hot chocolate before retiring for the night. By the time we went to bed, it was past 1:00 a.m.

During the night, I awoke to a gurgling sound. Louis was struggling to breathe. I quickly put on my robe and, disoriented, couldn't find the elevator and started shouting for help. Within a short while, the medics arrived, and I accompanied Louis in the ambulance to the hospital, where he was rushed into the emergency room.

Shortly thereafter, the doctors entered the waiting room and informed me that my dear, dear husband, friend, business partner, and hero had passed away from a heart attack at age sixty-four.

CHAPTER THIRTEEN

Finding Purpose through Hadassah

*Everybody can be great because
anybody can serve.*

—MARTIN LUTHER KING, JR.

𝒥 couldn't speak for twenty-four hours after Louis's passing. I was shattered. We had plans and ambitions that were no longer attainable. My rock and my partner was gone, and I was heartbroken.

Louis died on the Jewish holiday of *Simchat Torah*, the day when the last verse of the Five Books of Moses is read, the Torah is complete, the chapters ended. It is also when the cycle restarts with the first verses of Genesis and the formation of our wondrous world of which the Almighty "saw that it was good."

For me, only the end of the chapter was obvious. I couldn't contemplate a future at that moment, let alone one that was good.

My niece, Sandy, came up to Reno to assist me. I was being attended to and consoled by a chaplain in the hospital, as I was suffering from extreme shock.

In an attempt to overcome this devastating loss, I vowed to keep myself as busy as possible. Once I got started, I didn't leave myself time to wallow in my grief.

I collected and donated all of Louis's sports trophies and memorabilia to the Maccabi organization in Israel. As a result, there is a Trips Bowling competition named for Louis Krasner in the Maccabi Village in Ramat Gan. I later memorialized Louis at the Menachem Begin Heritage Center in Jerusalem through a legacy gift.

I became very active in local Jewish life, ultimately becoming involved with Maccabi, Hebrew Home, Congregation Beth El, South African Jewish American Committee (SAJAC), New Life Club, the Jewish Community Relations Council, the Soviet Oppressed Jewry Council, and Hadassah, The Women's Zionist Organization of America, Inc. (HWZOA)

When I arrived in the United States, I was looking to join an organization that would fulfill my Zionist aspirations. I was invited to a meeting of the San Diego chapter of Hadassah. The keynote speaker, Dr. Mary Pilch, a well-known professor at San Diego State University, gave a captivating description of Hadassah and its history, values, and objectives. This presentation made a huge impression and convinced me to become an integral part of the local chapter of Hadassah.

Not only was Hadassah the largest Jewish organization and the largest women's organization in the United States, but it had created and offered a unique structure of social services that continues to create realities out of dreams.

When I think of Hadassah, I think of healing, teaching, building, training, planning, and planting. It is a respected organization that is representative of Jewish women and values around the world. Each Hadassah project is an expression of the fulfillment of the Zionist dream and Zionist reality. In 1948, we fought for the establishment of the State of

Israel. Today, we have to fight for continued existence and safety. Israel has but one loyal ally, and that is us—*klal yisrael*—the entire Jewish people.

For several years, I served as president of the largest San Diego chapter of Hadassah and before that as program chair. In 1989, I became president of the Pacific Southwest Region of Hadassah. To this day, I have continued my commitment to the Hadassah organization, which for more than a century, has extended its hand to all, regardless of race, religion, gender, or country of residence.

I recall with great pride attending the Friday night dinner at a Hadassah National Convention in the mid-1980s. It was one of more than thirty national conventions I have attended. The feeling of togetherness and camaraderie on this night was hard to describe. Three special ladies were honored, each of whom was ninety years of age or older.

I was so inspired during this event. Everyone spoke so eloquently about their experiences with Hadassah. They talked about the time before the birth of Israel. And they talked about the days after the State of Israel was established. They painted pictures of the rescue of children in the beginning of Youth Aliyah.

All of the honorees had the pleasure of meeting Henrietta Szold, the founder of Hadassah. Hearing their remarks left me with a strange but wonderful feeling.

A tiny but beautiful woman got up to speak first. She stood maybe four feet eleven inches tall. Judith Epstein, who had served as national secretary of the organization and as president from 1937 to 1939 and from 1942 to 1947, was a member of Hadassah for seventy-two years until she died on my birthday in 1988.

She started her speech quietly, and then the volume of her voice increased as she went along. Her remarks that evening were so inspiring.

Then, Violet "Lola" Ingeborg Else Kramarsky, née Popper, addressed the gathering. She served as national president of Hadassah from 1960 to 1964. Lola began her speech with the following words: "I was not born Jewish."

She then told the story of being born in Hamburg, Germany, marrying Siegfried Kramarsky, and fleeing the rise of Hitler and anti-Semitism in 1932. The family settled in New York from the Netherlands in 1940, aided by Dr. Chaim Weizmann, a family friend who became the first president of Israel. After some years, she was converted by Rabbi Stephen Weiss,[48] an uncle of her late husband. She threw herself into the work of Hadassah's Youth Aliyah program, rescuing and rehabilitating displaced Jewish children. She had been working for Zionism and the Jewish people ever since. Our sages tell us a convert is regarded like one of us and even more so. Their commitment to Judaism, our purpose, and our people is because of their choosing. And that is to be greatly admired.

It was such a thrill to spend my ninetieth birthday in Israel in 2012, celebrating the one hundredth anniversary of Hadassah. It was my thirty-fifth visit to Israel. Walking through the streets of Jerusalem with two thousand joyous fellow Hadassah celebrants was so heartwarming. We sang and listened to the sound of locals blowing the shofar, welcoming the visitors to the holy city.

Tears streamed down our faces as we walked to the Safra Square, where Shimon Peres, president of Israel at the time, delivered a speech dedicating the new Sarah Wetsman Davidson Hospital Tower at Hadassah Hospital Ein Kerem, a state-of-the-art medical facility that Hadassah built and donated to the State of Israel. Later, I attended Hadassah's prestigious Founders Dinner.

Amid all the celebrations, I managed to spend some quality time

---

48   Stephen Samuel Wise (born Weisz; March 17, 1874–April 19, 1949) was an American Reform rabbi and influential Zionist leader.

with my Israeli family and friends. I shared a memorable Shabbat dinner with cousins in Herzliya, made all the more special when my youngest son, Milton, both shocked and delighted me by arriving all the way from California, just as I was about to perform the blessing over the Friday night Shabbat candles.

"She almost collapsed when she saw me," recalled Milton. "My cousin had to hold her up. It was very emotional for her. That was one of the few times I had an impact on my mother. Unfortunately, it nearly killed her."

Equally impactful for Milton was a visit we made to Hadassah Hospital on that trip.

"When my mother walked in the door, it was almost as if she worked at the hospital," said Milton. "Everybody knew her. It was amazing."

This was family, this was home, this was Israel—the place I loved and had learned to love since my early childhood. This was *shalom bayit.* I was at peace in this home.

As my flight departed Ben Gurion airport in Tel Aviv and the realization set in that I might never return to the Holy Land, the memories came flooding back. I recalled my work in Stockholm as part of the World Jewish Congress to secure the United Nations vote for the establishment of Israel and contemplated some of my previous trips to Israel. I was reminded of 1958, when I stepped off the plane from South Africa onto Israeli soil for the very first time. I cried in appreciation to the Almighty for allowing me to experience this day. I was reminded of my visit in 1981 to the Western Wall while attending the first World Gathering of Holocaust Survivors in Jerusalem. It was there that the participating survivors pledged, "The Holocaust will never happen again."

In many respects, my commitment to and involvement in Hadassah is a reflection of my Jewish values. We share a common goal of bettering humanity, sharing the dream of a happy and healthier future, and ministering through kindness, one person at a time, irrespective of race or creed.

Hadassah is a volunteer organization that inspires a passion for and commitment to its partnership with the land and people of Israel. It enhances the health of people worldwide through its support of medical care and research at the Hadassah Medical Organization's two hospitals and research centers in Jerusalem.

I'm proud to say that on all thirty-five trips I have made to Israel over the years, I have visited Hadassah Hospital in Jerusalem. Hadassah cares for all without discrimination. It is a community—a family of like-minded individuals seeking peace and camaraderie. First and foremost, it is committed to Israel and the Jewish people.

I've received many Hadassah awards, including the Woman of Distinction Award, Book of Builders Award, President's Award, and Citation for Distinguished Leadership and Service to the Jewish People. I introduced the "Keeper of the Gate" program and helped establish Hadassah's Nurses and Health Professionals Council, and the Persian Women's Hadassah group in San Diego, as well as helping to found the Hadassah San Diego Attorneys Council.

Over the years, I have been deeply honored and humbled to be recognized by various other organizations for my community service and philanthropic efforts. These include the Woman of Valor Award from Congregation Beth El in La Jolla, California (2017); Fanny Krasner Lebovits Appreciation Day from the San Diego City Council (February 11, 2017); and an honor from the California State Assembly on Holocaust Memorial Day (April 8, 2013).

CHAPTER FOURTEEN

Another Blessing

When one door closes, another opens.
—ALEXANDER GRAHAM BELL

Jenny and I lived on opposite coasts, but our lives seemed intertwined and had remarkable parallels. Jenny's husband, Roma Isakson, passed away in 1980 at age fifty-three, exactly three months before my husband Louis died.

In December 1982, I married Morris Lebovits, a United States Navy commander and aeronautical engineer. Six months earlier, Jenny had married Eli Sommer.

Morrie got along splendidly with my sister and her new husband. Every December, we would spend a month in Florida with Jenny and Eli. We did that until the year Morrie became ill.

I first met Morrie at his grandson Josh's *bris*, a Jewish circumcision ceremony, in May 1981. Josh is now a successful lawyer in San Francisco. How time flies! Morrie had just returned from his first trip to Israel with his sister, Gertrude. He was so enthused and energized by that trip. He became a staunch Zionist after that experience.

Meanwhile, I was attending the bris at the invitation of family on the in-law side. My son Milton was married at the time to Robin Nelson, whose sister, Cathy, was married to Morrie's son, Dr. Marc Lebovits, an ear, nose and throat specialist and surgeon. Ruth Nelson, Robin and Cathy's mother, had wanted to introduce me to Morrie after he and his wife had separated. Ruth thought we would be a good match. We were introduced, we enjoyed each other's company, and we became friends.

I knew Morrie was someone special when, after returning to New York from a trip to Israel and South Africa, he flew in from San Diego to surprise me. Jenny knew about it and didn't tell me.

In October 1982, Morrie took me out for dinner to the Westgate Hotel in San Diego to celebrate my sixtieth birthday. He proposed, kind of, by presenting me with a gold Cross pen-and-pencil set. He waited for his divorce to be finalized before asking me to marry him. We were married December 14, 1982.

Morrie's father had moved from Hungary to Los Angeles on his own in the 1930s. He lived and worked there a few years before being able to afford to bring his wife and six children to America. They had two more children, with Morrie being the youngest. Morrie's father had an appliance business. He manufactured and serviced ice cream refrigerators or coolers in the stores. Morrie loved to accompany his father on his service rounds because he would get as much ice cream as he could devour.

Morrie was the most wonderful person you could ever meet. We never had an argument. He was so even tempered that you could never get mad at him. He wasn't particularly outgoing, but he was extremely knowledgeable and highly educated. Everybody liked him.

"They were an excellent fit," said Marc. "Fanny is outgoing and in charge. She made all the arrangements and plans. My father was very quiet, very intelligent, and thoughtful. Being the youngest child in a family where most of his siblings were female, he was used to being led around and told what to do. That fit his makeup perfectly."

Morrie was so willing to support me and was so proud of my commitment to various causes. He supported everything I did for Israel and the community. He was delighted to accompany me to Tel Aviv in 1985 for the fortieth anniversary of the fall of the Reich.

Together, Morrie and I blended our growing families. I was thrilled to add a devoted stepson, Marc, and his lovely wife, Cathy, to the family. Cathy was a vivacious, outgoing, and intelligent woman with whom I immediately bonded. I was so saddened when she passed away from cancer in 2015.

I am very close with Marc, along with his sons, Matt and Josh, and his grandchildren. They are part of my family. Marc noticed my commitment to family immediately.

"Fanny expected everyone to be at her home for Shabbat meals," said Marc. "Everyone was supposed to be at everyone else's family *simchas* (Jewish festive occasions). Fanny was the driving force. You knew what was expected, and you performed. You can't say no to Fanny. And if you do, she doesn't hear it. She'll ask you five times until she gets the answer she wants."

Morrie and I traveled extensively. We toured the Far East with a group of about twenty-five people from Hadassah. We had a Jewish guide, and during this adventure we went to some unexpected Jewish locales. One day, we met an Asian Jewish shopkeeper in Tokyo. He had a music shop downstairs. Meanwhile, upstairs he had a collection of his calligraphy. Included in this collection were some beautiful Passover *Haggadahs*, Jewish texts that set the order for the Passover seder. We were so impressed. It was so unusual to

Fanny and Morrie at Milton and Stephanie's wedding

discover this in Japan. This was one of the highlights of our trip.

On another occasion, Morrie and I traveled to Hungary to visit his father's old home. Morrie couldn't speak Hungarian, but I could understand the language a little. There had been many Hungarians in the concentration camps, so I had managed to pick up a few phrases here and there.

On that trip, we also visited Morrie's first cousin in Michalovce, Czechoslovakia (Slovakia since 1993). The city is located on the shore of Lake Sirava, on the border with Ukraine. His family had told him about his cousin, although Morrie had never met him before. When his cousin opened the door, I immediately knew they were related. Morrie didn't look very Jewish, and neither did his cousin. They both had blue eyes, and from one glance, you just knew they were family.

What was striking to me was how two cousins who had the same grandparents and looked so similar could have led such different lives, all based on their parents' decisions before the war on where to live and build their legacy. It again reminded me of how fortunate we are to have found our way to the United States.

We also visited Budapest on that trip. We were so impressed by the museums in Budapest. And we toured the famous Dohány Street Synagogue, the largest synagogue in Europe.

Family photo in 1992 celebrating Fanny's 70th birthday – Morrie and Fanny in third row center

Morrie was very proud of his grandchildren and my children and grandchildren. We had a warm and loving family. My children were his children, and in return, my children thought the world of him.

"We are so delighted to have Morrie in the family," Harold often said.

Sadly, in 1995, Morrie was diagnosed with cancer of the esophagus. He suffered for more than a year. After they operated on him, Marc came out and said they got everything out and that he'd be OK. But it wasn't OK. I think Marc just wanted to make both of us feel better.

Morrie passed away in September 1996. He was a wonderful man.

I still have Marc and his children and grandchildren, my great-grandchildren. We are cemented as family, no different than my biological kids. And now we have Shana, Marc's wonderful wife, whom he married in 2016. She has been a delightful addition to the family.

I cherish the heartfelt remarks from Marc at my 95th birthday party in 2017:

…Fanny always had time for us. Her presence in our lives changed the direction of the lives of myself and my children, being instrumental in inspiring one son, Josh, to make Aliyah and join the IDF, and another son, Matt, to become an Orthodox Jew, and setting me on a path of deeper understanding and love of Judaism at my late stage in life. And to this day, 21 years after my father passed, she, and her children and grandchildren—clearly all molded by her—have kept my family as part of their family.

As I reflect back on the privilege of having been married to three wonderful but very different men, I contemplate how I changed as their partner during our life together.

Monya and I shared a relationship at the darkest of times as equal partners devoted to improving the community around us. It was far less about us and much more about them—the people around us—and surviving our respective traumas.

With Louis, I was his wingman, supportive in every way I could be to a most charismatic, talented man who was always happiest being at center stage. I worked with him; I played sports with him. Together we brought up wonderful children and built a loving home.

Morrie, conversely, preferred to be in the background. He could not have been more supportive of my family, my charitable and community pursuits, my desire to travel, and my commitment to tell my story as a means for future generations to never forget.

As noted American psychologist Abraham Maslow once wrote, "Our interpersonal style must be flexible. Otherwise…it is tempting, if the only tool you have is a hammer, to treat everything as if it were a nail."

In the more than twenty years since becoming a widow for the third time, I have utilized all these learned skills and attributes to lead a productive and fulfilling life. I remain committed to my communities. I am devoted to my family and try to inspire them to act with dignity while enjoying their own life journeys. And I continue to seek support from those willing and interested in sharing common interests.

I am convinced that life is a series of experiences, preparing body and soul for the next stage of our personal development. Enjoy the present, and learn from it!

CHAPTER FIFTEEN

Miracles

There are only two ways to live your life.
One is as though nothing is a miracle. The
other is as though everything is a miracle.

—ALBERT EINSTEIN

It may sound trite, but during the Holocaust I always believed I would survive.

It is astonishing what human beings can withstand—both physically and mentally. Where there is hope, there is faith. Where faith lives, miracles arise.

Whether it was faith, hope, or just plain denial, I remained steadfast that somehow, some way, I would survive that nightmare. "One day, I will be free," I kept telling myself. I reckoned if I said it often enough, it would come true.

Throughout my entire Holocaust days and since then, I have experienced many, many miracles. However, there are three distinct events that occurred during the Holocaust that I consider the greatest of the miracles. And each one also had a tragic element.

The first miracle occurred December 15, 1941—the first night of Chanukah—when we were removed from our homes in Libau. The Jewish population of nine thousand in Libau would soon be reduced to eight hundred.

After being transported to the women's prison, we were separated into different lines. Had the SS officer not ordered me out of one of the lines and interrogated me about my nursing background, I may not have been granted my release to go home, accompanied by my mother and my sisters.

My sisters, my mother, and I were saved from certain death. But my grandfather, aunts, and cousins all perished.

The second miracle took place on October 8, 1943—Yom Kippur night, the holiest night on the Jewish calendar—when we were transferred via cattle cars from the Libau ghetto to the Kaiserwald concentration camp.

We were separated into two lines. One line would survive, and the other would not. Once again, I was spared. Rather than being sent to my death, I was registered at Kaiserwald concentration camp and eventually transported to Riga-Reichsbahn labor camp. I was able to save my sister Jenny but tragically, I was unable to save my mother, Sarah, and my baby sister, Liebele. They were sent to the Riga ghetto for a few weeks and then transported to be gassed at Auschwitz.

The third miracle happened in the spring of 1945 while we were floating aimlessly on a barge for nine exhausting days. We feared we were all going to die. Had an Allied plane not bombed the barge and ignited a fire, forcing the SS to send distress signals to other German boats, we might not have been spotted, removed from the burning barge, and ultimately liberated.

Just eighty of us—from an initial boatload of six hundred passengers—managed to survive. My dear husband Monya had died the previous day of typhus and met his final resting place in the Baltic Sea.

On May 5, 1945, I was literally born again. Memory is the source of our strength.

I have learned that life is bittersweet. But one's perspective needs to focus on the positives and build on them. In this way, we honor those who are with us and those who are no longer with us but are forever etched in our memories.

Of course there were many more miracles that I experienced between 1941 and 1945. Just getting up each morning and making it through the day was a miracle in itself, never mind making it through the forced march from Burggraben to Stutthof, surviving typhus, and the harrowing journey on the barge. But there were confluences of events that aligned just perfectly, without which I, too, would have been a victim of the Holocaust.

Elie Wiesel once said, "In Jewish history, there are no coincidences."

Had I been assigned to the infirmary at Kaiserwald, Jenny and I would not have been ordered to clean houses and would never have received the bread that sustained us from the two kind *Feldwebels*.

Had I not been assigned to the hospital in Stutthof in April 1945 and had Jenny, Roma, and Monya not contracted typhus, we all would have been marched into the sea and shot or killed in other ways.

Had the ambulance I was traveling in not been stopped by the British chaplain and his translator, Michael Neville, I probably would not have received the medical care I needed to survive my illness.

Had Captain Pritchard not taken a personal interest in my well-being, I probably would not have recovered to the point of being able to take advantage of a series of later miracles that have brought me to today.

Had I not spotted a black car with a Swedish flag on the road to Hamburg, I would not have met Mr. Wasserman and had the opportunity to go to Landskroner.

Had Rabbi Chasdan not seen my name on a list of refugees in quarantine, I would not have worked at the World Jewish Congress in Stockholm. (For that matter, had our parents not vacationed near each other years earlier, Rabbi Chasdan would not have recognized the name!)

Had Etta and I not crossed paths at the World Jewish Congress offices in Stockholm and had Etta and Louis not been guests at the Hurwitz wedding in Johannesburg, I may never have been reunited with Louis.

Had Louis not spotted a ring in a shop window in the Congo, there would have been no Star Jewelers business that provided the means for us to create a family and move to the United States.

Had I not met the Nelson family though my son Milton, I would not have met Morrie.

I could go on and on, but you get the idea. Everything happens for a reason. As if there is a grand plan for each one of us.

CHAPTER SIXTEEN

Generation to Generation

Whoever teaches his son teaches not
only his son but also his son's son—and
so on to the end of generations.

—TALMUD, KIDDUSHIN

My daughter-in-law Joy Krasner likes to relate the story of my grandson Ryan's determination during an athletic competition. During the most recent Ironman event in which he competed, Ryan had just completed the biking and swimming components of the grueling race. As he was about to commence the last leg of the event—the running segment—my grandson stumbled over to his mother and his former wife, Amy, and told them that he just couldn't continue. With their encouragement, along with Amy's willingness to run side by side with him for a short while, Ryan persevered and finished the race.

"That evening while we were celebrating Ryan's success, I asked him how he managed to muster the energy to finish," said Joy. "He told me that as he was nearing the end of the race, he felt spent, exhausted, and ready to quit. Then he thought of his grandmother. He thought of her resilience and strength through all of her experiences, and this provided him perspective on his momentary challenge, and her spirit drove him to the finish line."

It's heartwarming to know I have influenced my family in ways I couldn't have imagined possible.

In my role as matriarch of the Krasner-Lebovits family, it has been extremely gratifying to be able to impact successive generations. Witnessing my descendants share and embrace the values that are so important to me has brought so much satisfaction.

All of my nine grandchildren and thirteen great-grandchildren have attended Jewish day schools, often with great financial and lifestyle sacrifice from their parents. They also attended Jewish camps. My children and grandchildren have all married within the faith. My own children have followed Jewish traditions and are involved in the local community.

Milton Krasner and Marc Lebovits and their families have become observant Jews attending Orthodox synagogues. Harold was president of San Diego Jewish Academy for two years and served on the day school's board of directors for ten years. Shirley has been involved in numerous Jewish causes all her life.

I am so proud of my children, grandchildren, and great-grandchildren. They have given me so much joy and pleasure over the years! When she was a seventeen-year-old high school student, my granddaughter Kim

First wrote an essay for her honors English class about our special bond. Here is an excerpt from that essay:

Four generations at great-grandson Jordan's Bar Mitzvah

I stand in the synagogue watching my grandmother weeping as she prays. It is Yom Kippur, the Day of Atonement and a day of remembrance. I am Jewish and to me Yom Kippur has a special significance.

Surrounded by my family and friends, I begin to reflect over the past year. Where am I coming from and where am I truly going? But, slowly my thoughts wander back to my grandmother. Yes, Yom Kippur is the Day of Atonement, but personally it is more so a day of remembrance. My grandmother is a survivor of the Holocaust. To me, her tears in the synagogue become her story, her nightmare, her passage of regrowth, and my heritage.

I vividly remember the day she sat me down and told me her life story. It was a fascinating story of bravery and utmost horror.

My grandmother Fanny is a survivor of the Holocaust. She has had a great impact on my life, teaching me not only about my heritage, but about the meaning of life.

Although I can never forget even the most insignificant detail of her story, the sadness in her face, or the disgust in her voice, one profound statement has forever been ingrained in my mind: "When we are flat on our backs, we can only look up."

My grandmother has been my greatest inspiration. Her grandparents, her parents, and her sister were killed by the Nazis. She lived through the hardest of times and saw death not far in the distance, yet when her entire life seemed to crumble around her she refused to give up. She taught me that determination and courage can lead one down the road to success.

So, for me, Yom Kippur is not only the day in which I ask for forgiveness, it is a day I link directly with my heritage. As sundown approaches, Yom Kippur quickly comes to a close. The blowing of the shofar, a ram's horn, marks the end of a long day. The shofar evokes feelings in me of the successful passage from sin to repentance, from death to life.

I love you, Granny Fanny!

—Kim

March 16, 1992

I believe that each of us has an influence on future generations. I view myself as an important conduit for instilling values and traditions in my grandchildren to enable them to pass them on to future generations long after I am gone.

My granddaughter Lindy Rinkey, who was out of town and unable to attend my ninetieth birthday in 2012, sent me this heartwarming note:

Dear Granny:

You mean more to me than words can describe. I feel so honored to be your granddaughter. If it were not for you, your courage, and your strong-minded personality, we would not be here today. You survived the unthinkable. You are truly the backbone of our family. I hope to pass on to my family at least half of what you have passed on to me. Your determination, your unwillingness to give up, and your love for Israel and the Jewish community is remarkable. You have taught me the importance of family. I promise you that I will pass on the Jewish religion. I will do whatever it takes to give my children a Jewish education, Shabbat dinners, and all the holidays. Most of all you have taught me to be a fighter. To fight for what I believe in and to never give up. You fought for your life, your family and the Jewish religion, and I promise to continue your fight and hopefully pass it on to three more generations as you have done. I love you so much.

　　—Lindy

𝓘 am fortunate to have two marvelous daughters-in-law in Joy and Stephanie Krasner. Do we see eye to eye all the time? Of course not.

Stephanie, Milton's wife, is a pediatric nurse practitioner, a registered nurse, lactation specialist, and surgical nurse. She has for years been by my side in a caregiving way in so many respects—driving, fetching, doing, supporting. Stephanie has always encouraged her two wonderful sons, Ari and Daniel, to call their grandmother on Shabbat, birthdays, and holidays.

And it was Stephanie who encouraged Milton to surprise me in Israel on my ninetieth birthday. What a wonderful surprise that was! Milton is my baby, and I am so thankful for his beautiful relationship with Stephanie.

Joy, Harold's wife, also comes from a kind and compassionate family. When Joy and I first met, her father had just passed away. She was devastated. And she was exceptionally close to her mother. As a result, she was reluctant to leave South Africa in 1978 because it would mean leaving her mother behind. As a trained speech therapist, she would find her accent to be a detriment to professional growth in the US.

Joy has been a tremendous asset to Harold. She is strong minded, has worked diligently in their jewelry business, and has beautifully brought up their children, Stacy and Ryan. Both are committed to Judaism, either culturally or religiously. In fact, Stacy met her husband, Danny Varon, at Camp Ramah, a Jewish summer camp, and the couple, together with their children (my great-grandchildren), Ella and Hayley, are more observant than Harold, Joy, or me.

Both Stephanie and Joy consider me to have had a positive influence on their children and grandchildren, especially when it comes to their faith. What more could I want to hear from daughters-in-law?

Then there's my dear son-in-law, Howard First. He's been part of the family so long—he and Shirley have been married since 1971—that he feels as comfortable as an old shoe. Or, in his case, a moccasin. Over the years, Howard has been a great source of wisdom, strength, and guidance. I can always turn to him in times of need. He is a valued sounding board for me in my decision making. I have enormous trust in Howard. As an example, when I moved into my current condominium, he orchestrated the purchase, then organized the move while I was with my sister in Florida so that when I returned, every item was in exactly the same place as it had been in my prior apartment. He always comes through!

Yes, I am indeed blessed.

$\mathcal{I}$ am just another proud grandmother—proud of each and every one of my grandchildren for their values and commitment to their Jewish heritage, to excellence, and to healing the world.

Whether it's Ari Krasner or his brother, Daniel, working as students at the San Diego Food Bank, fighting the BDS (Boycott, Divestiture, and Sanctions) movement against Israel on campuses in Washington or the San Francisco Bay area, or going to Israel on youth programs; their cousin Stacy working to assist children as a speech therapist; or her husband, Danny, fighting human trafficking as an assistant district attorney in Orange County, they are all doing their part to improve the world for everyone.

Lindy followed in the footsteps of her uncle Harold by winning a gold medal in tennis at age fourteen at the Maccabi Games. (Harold won silver medals at two consecutive Maccabi Games.) Meanwhile, Lauri has blazed new ground in marketing at a senior level at CBS.

Most gratifying of all, though, is that the grandchildren are sacrificing, like their parents before them, to provide their children with a solid education in Jewish studies and values.

At one time or another during our lives, we've all held on to secrets. Whether it's been to protect others or to protect ourselves, we make conscious decisions to keep certain aspects of our life under wraps. Of course, the longer we hold on to those secrets, the more difficult they become to divulge. I once read that the scariest thing about secrets is what they want—they want out. Once we finally make the decision to share that secret, we achieve a liberation of sorts.

My children did not know I had been married to someone before their father. I agonized over divulging this secret. Finally, in conjunction with writing this book and in trepidation about their response, in December 2017, seventy-two years after his passing, I told them about my relationship with Monya Kaganski. I intentionally use the word *passing* because the Talmud tells us that a person is only dead when the memory of him has also died.

It was difficult for my children to understand why I had withheld this information. I just didn't want to create additional complexity and questions about a period in my life that was painful to recollect. It was something I just wanted to put behind me. I wanted for myself and my family to be normal and not to be defined by the events of the Holocaust.

As a leader of the Jewish Council in the Libau ghetto, Monya masterfully dealt with the psychological and services needs of the community.

Over the three-plus years we were married, Monya and I were mainly separated. While I provided medical services in the makeshift emergency hospitals at the camps, Monya was assigned to various duties in the labor camps. Of course, barracks in the camps were segregated, so we seldom even saw each other. The exceptions were on the boat to Danzig, where I suffered terribly from seasickness; at Burggraben, where we slept on the dirty floor without any coverings with fifteen hundred other inmates traveling back to Stutthof from Stolp; and in the infirmary in Stutthof, where Monya began his fatal battle with typhus. In spite of this extensive separation, we maintained an intense caring and devotion for each other.

I am privileged to have an opportunity to include a thorough description of Monya Kaganski, an outstanding individual who has no other means of recognition, as his whole family perished in the Holocaust. He was an individual whose presence, even when he wasn't present, gave me additional strength and a reason for hope during the war years. Monya was someone whom I and so many others admired.

When I finally told my children about Monya, they all responded in the same manner: "Why haven't you told us before?"

It did not upset them to learn about this part of my life; they only wondered why it took so long to find out.

In May 1945, I was physically liberated from the horrors of the Holocaust. In December 2017, I was emotionally liberated from a secret I had kept from my children all their lives.

Monya helped many individuals and families with issues they faced during the German occupation. He saved many lives in so many different ways. More than forty years after the war, I received a letter from Edward Anders, who became a brilliant scientist and professor of chemistry at the University of Chicago. After retiring to San Francisco, he authored a memoir of his youth, including the Soviet and German occupations of Latvia. Anders (whose original name was Alperowitz) wrote a thank-you letter to me in acknowledgment and appreciation for what Monya Kaganski had done for him as a boy in Libau.

Edward was a child of interfaith parents. *Mischling* was the German legal term used in Nazi Germany to denote those of both Aryan and Jewish ancestry. With the Anders family facing internment in the Libau ghetto, Monya had used his connections and eloquent legal training and experience in arranging with the German authorities for the family not to be considered Jewish so they could thus escape ghetto life. Edward and his mother eventually immigrated to the United States.

Only much later did I discover that Anders survived by a lie conceived by his father in desperation to save his wife and two sons, Georg and Edward. The story was that his wife, Erica, was a German foundling raised by a Jewish couple after she was "discovered on their doorstep with a note bearing only her first name and a cross, indicating she was a Christian." [49]

This made Edward and Georg half-Jews under the Nuremberg laws and merely second-class citizens rather than total outcasts at the time. But there arose another hurdle in August 1940, when the police required all residents to recertify their passports. To prove that they were half-Jews, they had to produce a certificate from the Jewish Council that they had never belonged to the Jewish religion.

"Fearing savage German reprisals, the head of the two-person Council declined, as both my brother and I were circumcised, had Bar-Mitzvahs, and never attended school on Jewish holidays," wrote Anders. "The other member, the outstanding young lawyer Monya Kaganski, came up with an ingeniously evasive formulation: Adolf Alperowitz, father of George and Eduard Alperowitz, does not belong to the Jewish congregation."

"That was true. My father had resigned from the congregation some years before after the death of my grandfather. The German official who received this statement was intellectually no match for Monya and failed to see through the calculated ambiguity. He granted the Alperowitz's a three-month exemption from Jewish status, which incredibly was renewed by other officials seven more times until late 1943. Miraculously the last

---

49   Edward Anders, *Amidst Latvians During the Holocaust*, Occupation Museum Association of Latvia, Riga, 2011. p. 49.

official, though leaving the family without protection, never notified the SD as was his duty."[50]

And so Monya's cleverly worded letter allowed Anders to avoid being subjected to the fate of other Jews.

Edward Anders's father and twenty-four other relatives perished in the various *Aktions* in Libau. Later, his brother Georg came down with typhoid. He was hospitalized, contracted diphtheria, and died in Latvia.

Edward and his mother managed to bluff their way through the horrific years of the German occupation. Eventually, they immigrated to the US in 1949, and Edward Anders was appointed a professor at the University of Chicago in 1955.

$\mathscr{I}$ cannot help but mourn the thought that so many brilliant Jewish minds were extinguished by the Nazis and wonder how different the world's frontiers in science, medicine, and the arts might be today if they and their offspring had survived and used their talents to heal and improve a fractured world.

I am reminded of the testimony in the war criminals case about when the Germans, at 9:00 p.m. on the very day they occupied Libau, June 29, 1941, ordered the tenants of Villa Minkeowskai in Witterstraße to line up in the courtyard. Walter Hahn, a Jewish refugee from Austria, eminent composer and the director of the Libau Opera, was a tenant and stepped forward when the Germans asked whether any of the tenants were emigrants from the Reich. He was shot on the spot.

To show further contempt, they ordered that his body be buried next to the garbage cans. What a waste of true talent. Oh, what could have been! These incidents, this waste of talent and brainpower, occurred millions of times.

---

50   Personal communication with Edward Anders, July 2018.

I've always had a special relationship with Jenny. It's only natural in that we were the lone members of our family to survive the war.

To this day, we have remained as close as sisters can be, geographical distance aside. We talk on the phone every day. In some respects, Jenny has always revered me. I was the older sister—domineering and protective.

She lived for my letters from South Africa, so much so that her sibling commitment occasionally became an issue of contention within her own family. But the fact is I was just as devoted to Jenny, and we have remained the closest of friends.

We have poured our hearts out to each other and have been more than best friends. We've loved each other, and we've aggravated each other. To Jenny's daughters, it sometimes seemed as if "their mother and aunt's blood ran through the same vein."

Jenny's kindness, love, and devotion to me have never waned. After Roma's passing and after she remarried Eli Sommer (and after I married Morrie Lebovits), Jenny would invite us to their home in Florida for four weeks each year. Among our many activities together, we would go to the condo complex weekly dance club. Jenny always insisted that Eli dance with me as well.

Eli was a kind, devoted, and genuinely nice man. He loved sports, and his two sons were like brothers to Jenny's two girls, all close in age. They formed an ideal nuclear family. Eli was as wonderful a brother-in-law as I could have wished for. Eli, too, was a survivor, having been sent to concentration camps from his hometown of Tarnów, Poland. At one time, he was the Polish table tennis champion. Eli passed away in March 2015.

When Eli took his last breath and was at peace, Jenny, Eli's children, and Jenny's two children were at the apartment with him. Sandy recalls that Eli was covered and wrapped on a gurney, which was carried through the doorway of the apartment.

She recalls her mother saying, "Isn't that so beautiful. He is being carried out like a king."

Despite their observant childhoods, there was little religion in Jenny and Roma's home. They were culturally very Jewish, and being Jewish was extremely important to both Roma and Jenny, but they were nonreligious. They emerged from the camps as nonbelievers.

Jenny once told her daughter, Sandy, "I prayed to God in heaven. I asked Him why I deserved this, and I never received an answer. Nobody helped me."

Since the war, Jenny has taken no comfort from prayer or religion. She got by with love and grit from giving and by displaying kindness to others.

Growing up with Roma and Jenny as parents, Eileen and Sandy were inundated, even "suffocated" by the ever-present cloud of the Holocaust hanging over their parents. With strong Jewish identity at home, the girls grew up with limited formal religious education or practice. Their parents' friends were almost all Holocaust survivors, and conversations were dominated by their history of victimhood and hate for their oppressors.

Personality-wise, Jenny and I couldn't have been more different, as noted by Jenny's daughter, Sandy.

"My mother is a simpler woman than Fanny," said Sandy. "Accomplished in her own right as a homemaker, she is both fully invested and dependent on her family. She was a middle child, nonconfrontational, a people pleaser, and a giver. She has a joie de vivre that won't quit! Though anxious at times, she is uncannily strong. A self-described follower, a foot soldier, willing to be led—mostly by Fanny.

"Fanny is a brave, bold leader, a doer. She is highly intelligent and purposeful. Fanny is a lover of life. Her blue eyes so clear, sparkling, and full of intelligence and light. The light of life. As if blessed by God."

Sandy, who regards herself as "having a Jewish soul," has faced life's challenges without religion but with an internal fortitude worthy of my admiration. Her ambivalence to Judaism as a religion led to a spiritual journey that has included meditation, Buddhism, Hinduism, and other explorations.

A self-proclaimed rebellious, independent child and woman, she became a successful entrepreneur and technology executive search consultant. She was married at age nineteen; had a daughter, Remi; and lost her husband Michael when she was just thirty-three years old. Sandy had two more children, Harry and Austin, from a second marriage, which ended in divorce after twenty-four years. Sandy cared for Harry, their eldest child, for many months while he was in a coma after a brain injury. None of Sandy's children have a desire to be involved in the local Jewish community.

Jenny's daughter, Eileen, moved to Johannesburg for a year of college and lived with us. She met and married Keith Levitt, Howard First's closest and best friend. Keith and Eileen have two children, Mark and Lauren. Neither is involved religiously.

Family, as you may have gathered by now, is an integral part of my life. I devote a great deal of time to cultivating those special relationships that I treasure so much. I regard personal communications with close and more distant relatives and friends as a gift to myself. A broad network of relationships provides support, affection, and continuity in one's life.

I'll never forget the warm hospitality I received from Louis's family when I arrived in South Africa. Until I got married, I lived in the home of Louis's brother and sister-in-law, Bernard and Jean Kay, along with their daughters, Marcia, Chamian, and Lucille. I remain in regular contact with the girls through weekly calls, even though they all reside in different corners of the globe.

I also maintain an extremely close relationship with Irving Krasner's daughter, Shirley, who now lives in Phillipsburg, New Jersey. Like my daughter Shirley, she also married a Howard—Howard Falk. There are so many cousins with whom I remain in contact in Israel, South Africa, Great Britain, and throughout the United States that I sometimes consider maintaining family connectedness as my full-time job. Thank goodness for global cell phone plans! This has enabled me to remain close with the Hirschhorn family in Israel, including cousins Manny and Ruthie Oren, Chana Gill, and Zvia Ravon. In fact on the occasion of my ninety-fifth birthday in 2017, Zvia wrote such a heartfelt poem in which she stated, "I wish we were sisters." I was so touched by her gesture along with so many other beautiful notes from around the world. The occasion was made extra special by the presence of my sister, Jenny, who flew in from New Jersey for the celebration.

I've never been one to have a fascination with numbers, but I have to admit I have witnessed some eerie coincidences in my life.

For example, four generations of my family have birthdays within a week of each other during the month of October. I was born October 27, 1922; my daughter, Shirley First, was born October 24, 1951; her daughter (my granddaughter), Lindy Rinkey, was born October 23, 1982; and her daughter (my great-granddaughter), Charli Rinkey, was born October 21, 2014.

And all my husbands died on the third day of the month. Monya passed away May 3, 1945; Louis passed away October 3, 1980; and Morrie passed away September 3, 1996.

Strange but true.

Some events and experiences in our lives simply have no plausible explanation. You just have to accept them for what they are. My son Milton, who possesses a tenor voice, is a founding member of the San Diego Jewish Men's Choir. He and his choir visited Omaha, Nebraska, in January 2018 to perform a concert along with the Omaha Symphony at Temple Beth Israel, a reform synagogue. The building had these unique stained glass windows interpreting God's biblical covenants with the Israelites. After the choir's performance, he sat in the audience listening to the inspiring music of the symphony. He experienced a moment that will be forever etched in his mind.

"The symphony was playing the theme music from *Schindler's List*," said Milton. "It is such a haunting tune. I had closed my eyes to appreciate the music. Then, when I opened my eyes at a potent moment during the violin solo, I noticed a flock of geese flying in formation outside the window of the temple. It was if they were flying free through the challenges of Jewish history emblazoned in the glass. I couldn't control myself. I started bawling. I immediately thought of my mother. It was incredibly powerful. I was thinking about the camps, and hearing that music and seeing that image just put me over the edge. It was a moment you think you will never experience."

CHAPTER SEVENTEEN

Time to Share, Time to Heal

Healing is a matter of time, but it is sometimes also a matter of opportunity.

—HIPPOCRATES

In 1994—fifteen years after immigrating to the United States and nearly fifty years after liberation—I explained in a note to my eldest child, Harold, why I had been reluctant to speak about my wartime experiences:

"Why didn't I tell you about my experience when you were young? Because when I lived in South Africa, and my husband was not a survivor, I wanted you to have a completely normal Jewish life like everybody else. In those days, the less we talked about it the better it was. I didn't want my children to know of my pain and what I went through."

Over the past few decades, I have visited numerous schools and colleges to talk about my Holocaust experiences. During these chats, I provide the students with a synopsis of the events that took place. I discuss some of the miracles that happened to me, and, when speaking to Jewish audiences, I reinforce that Israel must be a central focus for them. They are the ones who must continue to keep it safe. It's their obligation. Through a miracle, our homeland was given back to us. They need to know what we endured. This is what keeps me focused.

To this day, the first thing I do when I wake up each morning is reach for my iPhone. I have programmed the phone—yes, I am computer and smart phone literate—so that i24NEWS, the twenty-four-hour Israeli news network, pops up. I read the daily Israeli news headlines. Then I read the *New York Times* headlines. Throughout each day, I am conscious of current events in Israel.

I have made hundreds of speeches about my experiences, all the while imploring the world to never forget. I believe those who have survived this horrific episode have a fundamental responsibility to prevent such tragedies from happening in the future.

As I declared in an address to high school students in 2002, "As survivors—individually and collectively—we must imbue young Jews with an understanding of the significance of the two major events of our time. The Holocaust and the establishment of the State of Israel. They must perpetuate the memory of the Holocaust and all that we lost, even though it is difficult to comprehend the nature of this tragedy so many decades later. And as Jews, they must realize the importance of Israel to themselves and the future continuity of Jewish peoplehood."

The impact of my addresses to school groups and other organizations has been both humbling and overwhelming. I am so grateful for the comments and letters of support I have received from schoolchildren and the general public. Here is a sampling:

"It was really amazing to hear about those miracles. It gave me a sense of hope and faith, and it encouraged me to continue being a believer."

"I will remember your story forever and pass your experiences on to my children and grandchildren."

"You made me believe that miracles can happen."

"Your strength, wisdom, and courage can help turn evil to good and turn hatred to compassion."

"I admire you for being so brave and courageous. I will carry your story with me always."

"Your story will stay with me after the things I've read in textbooks have faded."

This heartfelt feedback further serves to underscore the necessity for me and other survivors to share our stories of the senseless atrocities of the Holocaust. It makes the difficult emotions I go through each time I tell my story and the sleepless nights I endure after delivering speeches well worthwhile.

During many of my speaking engagements, I close my remarks about my days of internment with these words: "In those dark days, we looked to the left for help, and there was no one. We looked to the right, and there was nobody. No one cared about us. Now, we don't have to look. We have the State of Israel to protect us."

My love for and commitment to Israel and all it stands for and protects in no way diminished my respect, admiration, and appreciation for the United States of America. To me it is the Jerusalem of the West, built on a covenant with God and between people as established in its Constitution. It is the beacon of respect for the individual and provides individual freedoms as described in its Bill of Rights. Of course there are always blemishes and missteps over time as in any country. Politics sometimes blurs the fundamental good intentions that drive our democracy. It is my home. And I am proud to call myself an American.

My message is to teach the generations not to hate. Teach people to love, to get along with each other. If people don't hate each other, events like the Holocaust won't happen again. I've seen so much evil, so many atrocities. But I find that it hasn't hardened me. On the contrary, it has made me a more compassionate person. And I've come out of the Holocaust with a belief that there is a lot of good in people. The whole world is not evil.

I share these thoughts Anne Frank wrote in her diary: "In spite of everything I still believe that people are really good at heart."

For me, the only way to fight evil is by telling people what happened during the Holocaust. There is so much hatred and jealousy in the world today. It's become a malady, a sickness.

How can you cure sickness like that? Personally, I believe you can only cure it through goodness, through love, and through compassion. You must show them the opposite of hate.

When I see somebody running for public office in 2018 who openly denies the Holocaust ever took place, it makes me feel terrible. But you have to take the high road. Otherwise, it's not worth living. We have to stand up against hatred to make the world a better place. And to make it better, you must exhibit love, compassion, and understanding.

I came out of the camps with a lot of strength and a lot of courage. I wasn't frightened to go and talk to people. I wasn't broken. I was strong. I went into the camps as a young, innocent girl. But when I came out, I could have been one hundred years old for all that I witnessed and lived through. I firmly believe in the proverb that says, "Fortune favors the brave." We all should face the world bravely.

$\mathcal{A}$ few years ago, out of the blue, I received a call from a lady in Atlanta. Her daughter, Lauren Rain, would soon be celebrating her bat mitzvah. Mother and daughter wanted to bring attention to the million and a half Jewish children who had perished in the Holocaust. In particular, they wanted to remember those who had been denied the opportunity to fulfill their rite of passage because of the Holocaust.

Lauren had been studying the Holocaust with her rabbi and had discovered that she could share her special day with a child who had perished in the war and had been denied a bat mitzvah. Lauren wanted a spiritual bat mitzvah "twin" and had researched and received information on several children through a program called Remember Us: The Holocaust B'nai Mitzvah Project.

One of the children happened to be Liebele Judelowitz, my baby sister. Lauren chose Liebele because she came from Latvia, as did Lauren's great-grandfather, Eli, who happened to be a shoemaker, just like Liebele's father. Both Lauren and Liebele came from a family of three girls.

Lauren's further research with Yad Vashem, the Holocaust memorial in Israel, indicated that I had registered Liebele in the database, and so they had tracked me down through my numerous citations in the Jewish community.

Over the next few months, Lauren spoke with me at length over the phone. Lauren learned about the beautiful little girl with straight blond hair and blue, blue eyes who was born on January 15, 1935, and killed on November 2, 1943. I proceeded to explain my own wartime traumas and history to the attentive twelve-year-old girl.

Lauren asked me what message I would like to share with the bat mitzvah girl's friends and family on her big day.

This is what I shared with her: "You should always believe in everything that is good. Be kind. Be compassionate. Follow the Ten Commandments, love your parents, treat your fellow man as you would want to be treated, and love Israel and protect it with all your might."

And so it came to be that more than seventy years after her cruel death, little Liebele Judelowitz was symbolically recognized, honored, and celebrated as a bat mitzvah in Atlanta, Georgia, United States of America, land of the free and home of the brave.

There is a building at Yad Vashem to memorialize and honor the 1.5 million Jewish children who were lost in the Holo-caust. It is dark and somber, with many little random flashing lights. As children's names are called out, they seem to come alive. Just like it was for my little sister Liebele when Lauren Rain mentioned her name at her bat mitzvah. *Zachor*, remember them, the young, the old, and the children.

Liebele at age 3

During the years of construction of the Holocaust Museum in Washington, DC, which began in July 1989 and ended in April 1993, a vast amount of effort was involved in planning and obtaining artifacts, information, and exhibits for the museum's content. During a trip to my beloved Hadassah National Convention in Washington with my husband Morrie, I received a call from a young man who worked in the museum. He asked me to come visit and tour the planning office for the museum.

I proudly recall seeing a huge model of the pending museum, registering as a Holocaust survivor, and being asked for an interview about my Holocaust experience to be included in an identification card for visitors to the museum. I was truly honored to become a charter member of the Holocaust Museum.

In 2013, on the twentieth anniversary of the opening of the Holocaust Museum, my four children accompanied me to a four-day celebration in Washington. It was incredibly moving and overwhelming to view this outstanding facility and contemplate it as a reminder to those millions who perished during that horrific period. Nearly eight hundred survivors attended and listened intently to the closing speeches by liberator General Dwight Eisenhower's daughter, followed by President Bill Clinton and then Elie Wiesel, who had been awarded the Nobel Peace Prize in 1986.

In October 2012, my granddaughter Lauri First Metross, with her husband, Ian, and their baby daughter, Alexis, visited the Holocaust Museum in DC as part of an East Coast vacation and business trip.

They arrived just in time. They hurried to the door, and the security guard allowed them in just before the museum was to close for the day.

They sped past the inscription that is etched in marble at the entrance to the museum: *Only guard yourself and guard your soul carefully, lest you forget the things your eyes saw, and lest these things depart your heart all the days of your life, and you shall make them known to your children, and your children's children. Deuteronomy 4:9.*

After entering the museum, Lauri and her family walked toward the elevator. They were stopped and encouraged by an usher to choose an identity card from a huge bowl they had passed at the entrance. The bowl was filled with passport-sized booklets describing a real person who lived through or died in the Holocaust. The purpose of the identity cards was to make the visitor experience at the museum more meaningful.

Each member of my granddaughter's party chose an identity booklet and then boarded the elevator. When they exited at the top floor, they began reading the heartbreaking stories contained in each booklet.

Lauri opened hers and began reading about a person named Fanny. As she continued to read, the background information seemed vaguely familiar.

Lauri rushed to the nearest restroom and frantically called her mother.

"Mom, the most bizarre thing happened to me," said Lauri. "I'm shaking right now. "

"What is it?" asked Shirley.

"I think I picked up Granny's passport," said Lauri. "Of all the passports in this museum, I think I picked hers. Tell me, was her family name Judelowitz?"

"Yes, it was," said Shirley.

"Is something terrible going to happen to me?" wondered Lauri. "What does this mean?"

US Holocaust Museum identity card

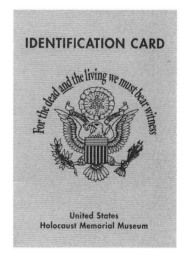

Front of identity card

"Nothing terrible is going to happen," said Shirley. "In fact, something wonderful will happen. Because you picked up your grandmother's passport, it means you have an obligation to teach your children about the

Holocaust and they have the obligation to teach their children about the Holocaust and so on and so on. That's why you picked up her passport."

"OK, I'm fine with that," said Lauri. "I'm going to call Granny right now."

And that she did.

Of the thousands of Holocaust victims' identity card booklets in the bowl, my granddaughter had chosen mine—complete with a summary of the information I had provided on my trip to DC more than twenty years earlier! What are the odds of that happening? Now her grandmother's horrific experience was "known to (her) children's children."

I enjoy a special relationship with all my grandchildren.

I often tell them, "When we are flat on our backs, we can only look up."

What I mean by that is when things don't go as you wish and you are feeling down, look toward the future with optimism and drive. And secondly, look toward God and understand that this is His will and in the grand scheme of your life, your current situation, no matter how difficult, is the exact prescription for the next step of your growth and progress. There will be light from this darkness. Find it!

Having been fortunate enough to have a platform, I will continue to speak out against hate at every opportunity.

On August 12, 2017, white supremacists—the Ku Klux Klan, neo-Nazis, and a selection of other right-wing extremists—held a "Unite the Right" demonstration in Charlottesville, Virginia, with heavy anti-Semitic overtones.

Marchers displayed swastikas on banners and shouted slogans like "blood and soil," a phrase drawn from Nazi ideology, and "Jews will not replace us." These right-wing extremists were met by counterdemonstrators, and violence ensued. A thirty-two-year-old woman was killed when a car was intentionally driven into the group of counterdemonstrators. I was aghast at the hatred I had witnessed more than seventy years after the Holocaust.

Within days, anti-hate rallies were held around the country. One of the first such rallies, called "Stand Up against Hate," was held at the Lawrence Family Jewish Community Center in San Diego just three days after the incident. Despite there being less than twenty-four hours to organize the event, the rally attracted an overflow crowd of seven hundred, comprising people of all religions and races. Speakers included rabbis, congressmen, and community leaders.

Just prior to the start of the program, one of the organizers asked me if I would say a few words during the presentation. I hastily scribbled down some notes on a scrap of paper, and when called upon as a survivor, I approached the lectern to a standing ovation.

These were some of my comments:

I personally know what it means to be discriminated against. To be a minority and to experience anti-Semitism, even today. But I always believed in the good of humanity, and I still do, and it has lit up many dark moments for me. We survivors continuously came face-to-face with death. Yet despair was not our response despite hopelessness. We created life out of a world of darkness. We remember the all-consuming evil we were forced to endure. But to remember is not enough. Deeds as well as thoughts are critical. We all have an obligation to instill in the current and future generations the understanding of what happens when prejudice and hatred are allowed to flourish. We must teach tolerance and understanding, for tolerance cannot be assumed. And we must make it clear that hate is never right and love is never wrong.

My remarks seemed to resonate with the audience, who embraced me with a long ovation at the conclusion of my speech. The response brought chills to a four-foot-ten-inch, soon-to-be ninety-five-year-old woman.

I realize that standing up against hate is not always easy, comfortable, or in some cases even possible. And one's reactions vary by circumstance.

When we lived in Libau, despite being protected by my parents, I experienced periodic hateful remarks such as being called a "dirty Jew" by other children, who were no doubt influenced by their parents or peer pressure. We lived with it passively. It passed, until it surfaced again. And then it came again, and eventually the hate, when given an outlet either by the Russians or the Germans, became pervasive. And then we had no voice. No means of standing up against hate.

The Libau killings. Fathers, brothers, sisters, mothers. The elderly, the young. No protest possible. No one to listen. Too late.

The ghetto hate. We just got on with our assignments. We actually took pride in our work despite the overwhelming hate. We never lost hope. We had no means of speaking out. Yes, the Jewish Council did what they could to negotiate, cajole, confer, debate, haggle, bribe, beg, and compromise with our captors. But, we had no leverage to speak out against hate in a meaningful way. We just carried on.

We were utterly helpless to stand up to the overwhelming hate in the concentration camps. Those who did died. Often they suffered in-comprehensibly cruel deaths.

Then I experienced otherworldly kindness in Sweden. At first we found the kindness difficult to accept, given what we had previously encountered. We appreciated and enjoyed the love and freedom we were shown. We didn't have to speak out. Or should we have spoken out? Hate continued in other countries. Visas were denied because of religion. Displaced persons camps in Europe were still filled. We had the opportunity to speak out, but we didn't.

I was shocked and distraught over the racism that was prevalent when I arrived in South Africa. But we didn't speak out because it was politically dangerous. We just wanted to get on with life. Again, the thing about hate is that, depending on its source—laws, practices, acceptable social behavior—it can be intimidating. Sometimes hate is subtler. Things like exclusion, jokes, or political objections to Israel may have anti-Semitic undertones. In the end, this hate, discrimination, reverse discrimination, and racism boils over, and society feels threatened by the disaffected, the hate perpetrators, or both. Then valuable human resources vote with their feet and leave the arena, fearing the consequences. And it's too late to speak up.

I have witnessed all these situations. I sometimes feel I have been wounded by hate and so now feel compelled to speak out while I can.

As Hillel the sage once said, "That which is hateful unto you, do not do to your neighbor."

And if I may add, use your voice to protest hate and encourage love, comradeship, and kindness.

I've always regarded myself as a strong and independent person. When I hear the term *emotional strength*, I see it as the ability to deal with the challenges and adversity in our lives and how successful we are in bouncing back from those setbacks. In that respect, I think I've demonstrated emotional strength throughout my life. To endure, overcome, and recover from the many traumatic experiences I've encountered along the way serves to reinforce that ideal.

We've never been to hell. We know the world such as it is, but we've never been in hell. In hell, you get burned. Those are the tales that we hear—that you burn in hell. Well, where I had been was hell, a living hell. And millions of people were burned in the hellish crematoria.

At the same time, I've learned that while reflecting on past experiences is important in that you can learn from them, it's just as important not to dwell on those experiences. This balance helps you maintain a positive outlook.

Granted, there are times when I'm alone and I feel sad. During those moments, my emotional strength is not what it should be. It's only natural. It's hard to remain strong all the time. Sometimes you feel you deserve to be pampered.

But just when I start feeling sorry for myself, I quickly realize how fortunate I am. I have a wonderful family—lovely children, incredible grandchildren, beautiful great-grandchildren. And I have friends and interests that I love and cherish.

Just after moving to America to settle near our children and enjoy our retirement, I lost my dear husband after thirty-one incredible years of marriage. Trying to cope after that terrible tragedy was so difficult.

But I picked myself up, thanks to my faith, my family, and my surrogate family—Hadassah. Keeping myself busy with philanthropic work and community service definitely helped me through my tragedy. I never had to seek professional help. I like to say I'm my own psychologist. My doctor keeps telling me that my mental health is incredible.

And of course, as you age, your body becomes a challenge at times. But somehow I have been provided with the tools to cope and fight back.

In 2012, I traveled to Sonoma, the wine country outside San Francisco, to attend the wedding of Howard First's niece, Carrie. A limousine was provided for the family to attend the pre-wedding rehearsal dinner. After dinner, while stepping into the limo, I slipped and ripped the whole front side of my left leg. I was bleeding profusely. I headed to the hospital in Santa Rosa, where I was told I would need a skin graft.

"No way," I said. "I am attending the wedding tomorrow, so bandage it up and give me some Tylenol!"

Heavily bandaged, I was present at the wedding the next day. I then spent the next six months healing and required regular dressing changes. I never did have a skin graft. I recovered the old-fashioned way!

More recently, I was driving my car and was involved in a major accident in which my sternum was crushed. My kids did not think I would make it. But I summoned all my strength and rallied. Although I was in hospital and at a physical rehabilitation facility for quite some time, I am fully recovered, but I don't drive anymore—under orders from my children!

My children say they marvel at the busy schedule I maintain. They tell me I have the energy of a thirty-year-old. I don't know about that, but I do know I have so much to live for and so much to do. And I don't like to miss out. I want to attend every lecture and every film.

They will often ask, "What else can you learn at your age?"

I tell them I learn something new every time I go to a lecture, read a book, or engage in conversation. It was Hillel who said, "He who does not increase his knowledge, loses it."

Overcoming tragedy—the Holocaust, the loss of loved ones—takes a lot of intestinal fortitude. If you're constantly consumed by your misfortunes, it creates a negative atmosphere for you and those around you. In my situation, the best antidote has been to keep busy and do good things for others. Life is filled with so much joy.

My faith has played a major role as well. I'm not a strictly observant Jew, but I believe strongly in a greater being. Certainly, my faith has helped me get through the difficult times. Faith is a source of strength and healing. It is said that healing after tragedy does not occur through increased acts of personal gratification. Healing happens through increased holiness. I take full responsibility for my actions and understand that I am accountable to a higher authority.

It also helps to find something fulfilling in your life. For me, it's very painful to talk to groups about my experiences in the Holocaust. But when I return home after addressing an assembly of schoolchildren and reflect upon it, I find it very gratifying. You have to look for positive things that bring you satisfaction. Certainly, when I talk about my experiences in the war, it's upsetting, and I cry. But maybe that's a good thing, and maybe it provides me some relief.

I've lived a life that's been bursting with emotional highs and lows. From humiliation at the hands of the Nazis to humanistic work at UNRRA and commitment at the World Jewish Congress, through a fulfilling business career and community involvement to a family life of joy interspersed with tragedy, I've tried to be generous with my time and exhibit personal kindness to all. Others' misfortunes were treated as my own, and my concerns were nobody's business.

I can relate to Rabbi Ron Schulman of Congregation Beth El in La Jolla, California, who stated in a 2017 sermon, "We can leave [decisions] up to others, feeling that we're not qualified to guide our own futures; worried that we won't be resilient enough to overcome any unintended consequences of our choices. Or, we can see in our lives the blessing of God's trust in us, a convergence of our best instincts and life's greatest opportunities. Aware that we can't know the future, we can still imagine its promise and potential." [51]

Mark Twain once said, "The two most important days of one's life are when you are born and when you find out why."

My initial purpose in life was clear—to help others. Nursing was a calling to me, and healing was my calling card, my mission. My purpose has been to help others attain *b'riut*, the health of body, soul, and intellect. My whole life has been about saving and improving the lives of others while maintaining a positive attitude driven by hope and belief.

There is a Hebrew expression, *gemilut chasadim*, bestowing kindness, that is often translated as acts of loving kindness. It is not just *tzedakah*, donations, monetary assistance for the poor. The essential characteristic is personal involvement and kindness to others. I hope I've lived by that example.

People will often approach me and say, "I'm so jealous of you, Fanny, for what you have. You have your family, your grandchildren, your great-grandchildren. And you love what you do."

That brings a smile to my face.

---

51   Rabbi Ron Schulman, sermon at Congregation Beth El in La Jolla, California, November 4, 2017.

CHAPTER EIGHTEEN

Upholding Moral Values

*The highest reward for man's toil is not what
he gets for it, but what he becomes by it.*

—JOHN RUSKIN, NINETEENTH-CENTURY BRITISH
POET AND SOCIAL COMMENTATOR

I think it's appropriate that this closing section of my story is chapter 18. That's because in Judaism, the word *chai* is numerically significant, and the number 18 is universally synonymous with this word. Numerically, the word consists of the eighth and tenth letters of the Hebrew alphabet, *chet* and *yud*, which add up to the number 18. Together, these letters form *chai*, which translated from Hebrew to English means "life."

For Jews, there is a need to leave a legacy to the Jewish people. Quite frankly, we are the ones who must look after ourselves. The world has shown that nobody else will look after us. When it comes right down to it, it's all up to us.

For those of us who survived the horrors of the Holocaust, it was difficult to share our experiences with loved ones. Often, we waited decades before opting to relive that nightmare.

In the view of Rabbi Lord Jonathan Sacks of London, England, who was chief rabbi of the United Hebrew Congregations of the Commonwealth for twenty-two years, it was a case of choosing to build one's future rather than sharing painful reminders of the past.

"Often, they did not talk about their experiences during the *Shoah*, even to their spouses, their children, and their closest friends," said Rabbi Sacks in an excerpt from a commentary published in November 2017. "This silence lasted, in many cases, for as long as 50 years. Only then, when the future they had built was secure, did they allow themselves to look back and bear witness to what they had suffered and seen. Some of them wrote books. Many of them went around to schools, telling their story so that the Holocaust could not be denied. First, they built a future. Only then did they allow themselves to remember the past. To survive tragedy and trauma, first build the future. Only then, remember the past."[52]

Every Yom Kippur, I sing a Yiddish song, "Eli, Eli—God, oh God, why did you forsake me?" at Congregation Beth El in La Jolla, California. The words of this song are so poignant and so meaningful. This was the song millions of Jews sang in concentration camps and ghettos and on their way to extermination. To me, it serves as a reminder that we must never

---

52   Rabbi Jonathan Sacks, Covenant and Conversation. November 6, 2017. The World's Oldest Man (Chayei Sarah 5778) http://rabbisacks.org/worlds-oldest-man-chayei-sarah-5778/

forget and must have faith in God and in the Jewish people's strength and continuity.

Oh God, Oh God
Why did you forsake me?
We are consumed by fire and flame.
We are universally despised and scorned.
Yet, no power on earth could turn us away.
From our holy Torah and your commandments.
God, oh God, why did you forsake me?
Day and night, my thoughts are only turned only toward you.
I heed with all your Torah and Ten Commandments.
Deliver me from danger as our fathers were delivered from evil decrees
Harken to my prayer and my lament
You and only you can ease the pain.
Hear O' Israel,
The Lord is our God.
The Lord is One.

𝓕𝑜𝓻 me, the Jewish High Holy days—from Rosh Hashanah to Yom Kippur—are especially meaningful. Not merely because our family spends time together, but also because these are the ten days during which our tradition tells us to pray for a favorable judgment, for life, laying bare our shortcomings and asking for forgiveness. There is one prayer in particular that we chant on Rosh Hashanah, a liturgical poem referred to as *Unetaneh Tokef* ("we shall ascribe holiness to this day"), during which every year I seem to sob, drawing the attention of my children and grandchildren.

This poem comes from Jewish apocalyptic literature, similar to many

Christian writings such as the *Dies irae*, "day of wrath," in the requiem mass. These poems describe the Day of Judgment for all humankind.

When we get to the words of the *Unetanah Tokef*,

On Rosh Hashanah it is inscribed,
And on Yom Kippur it is sealed.
How many shall pass away and how many shall be born,
Who shall live and who shall die,
Who shall reach the end of his days and who shall not,

my mind rushes to my deceased husbands, my parents, my dearest little sister Liebele, the seventy-nine members of my family who perished in the Holocaust, those others whom I witnessed die and disappear, and the millions who were killed at the hands of the Nazis merely because of their faith. I also recall my friends and family who have since passed on, and I wonder about my own mortality and the year ahead.

Our texts and commentaries describe how the light is hidden in the darkness. "Though I sit in darkness, The Lord is a light unto me." Had I never sat in the darkness, I would never have seen the light. Darkness is a source of light.

We all have a choice on how we lead our lives. My life has spanned three continents, each location representing its own unique challenges, hurdles, and triumphs.

When I celebrated my ninetieth birthday in 2012, I had this message for those in attendance: "Life had to go on. Live life to the fullest was my motto and still is. I love life and all that it stands for. I have lived a happy life. I have always considered the glass half full and not half empty."

The odds were definitely stacked against me and my sister. It has been reported that at liberation, just 176 Libau Jews survived the camps and 33 others were found hiding in Libau.[53] It was indeed a miracle that Jenny and I survived.

On June 9, 2004, Jenny traveled to Libau for the unveiling of the Liepāja Holocaust Memorial to honor the thousands of Liepāja Jews who died in the Holocaust and to honor the two hundred survivors.

In a message read at the memorial, Vaira Vike-Freiberga, president of Latvia, stated, "Today, standing here at the memorial site for the victims of Nazism, it is important for everyone to understand and evaluate the events of that time. What madness and hatred had seized people that caused them to destroy thousands of innocent fellow men?"

I survived the horrors of five Nazi concentration camps and a Jewish ghetto. I was one of a tiny percentage from my home country—about 1.25 percent of Latvian Jews—to survive the Holocaust. Sometimes I think maybe I was dreaming—that it was humanly impossible to survive something like that. How could I ever have survived it and remained normal—in a way, much more normal than people I meet in everyday life?

I've been told countless times that I demonstrated many examples of courage, responsibility, care, and commitment to others while I was interned.

People will often come up to me and ask, "Fanny, this incredible

---

53   *Latvia SIG* 10, no. 1 (October 2005).

strength and belief that you've exhibited throughout your life, where does it come from?"

The first time I was posed that question, I had to pause for a moment. But then it came to me. I believe it comes from my remarkable upbringing and my desire to uphold moral values. Values I hope I have passed on to my children, grandchildren, and great-grandchildren. Without that stable foundation instilled by my parents, I would have never found the strength, will, and fortitude to carry on.

I often wonder why I have been blessed with such a long life. Why have I experienced the highs and lows through almost a century? Is there a reason that I was born Jewish, was almost annihilated as a Jew, and have been fortunate enough to be the matriarch of a large Jewish family? What is the responsibility I have to myself, my family, my community, and humankind for these experiences?

I can only conclude that my obligation is to relay to others the life lessons I have learned, for them to contemplate and decide their own course. Some of the lessons I could impart—based on almost a century of life experiences—include these:

1. Have faith and believe in miracles.

2. Family is your most valuable asset. Protect it, nurture it, and influence it. Your impact lasts generations.

3. Show compassion and kindness for others.

4. Maintain a positive attitude, and exude confidence.

5. Perseverance and internal strength are the most important attributes in attaining objectives.

6. It is your obligation to take personal and communal responsibility for others and for moral causes. Stand up against hate.

7. Without a strong Israel, history will repeat itself. Do your part! Never again!

8. Learn about and understand your heritage. Gain valuable insights, and avoid the mistakes of the past.

9. Keep busy to lighten the trauma of tragedy.

10. There is a reason for everything that occurs. We just may not understand it in the moment.

Yes, I've overcome the struggles, pain, and tragedy of the Holocaust. I chose to become a nurse because I always wanted to alleviate pain and make people feel better. Resilience and a positive outlook have allowed me to live an extremely rich and fulfilling life.

Reflecting on my experiences, I attribute my survival to faith, a desire for life, and a belief in miracles. All of us have a purpose on this planet, and none of us can ever really know the magnitude of our impact on others. Even in the depths of my worst experiences, I never believed the world was evil. If I had believed that, I would not have had hope. Hope in Hebrew is tikvah, which as a Jewish value implies an expectation of outcome. With hope, there can be no equivocation.

I was so honored and humbled to receive the Woman of Valor Award at Congregation Beth El on February 11, 2017. I treasure the words in the printed program:

Fanny has made it her life's work to tell the story of her experiences so future generations learn and "never forget," trying to insure it never happens again. Through Fanny we learn about hope, miracles, and what the Jewish people have experienced, and we learn about resilience, caring, and love. Fanny's life has been one of playing her part in a holy nation, striving to be a light unto other nations, and doing all she can to repair a fractured world.

In accepting this prestigious award, I said, "Despite my experiences during World War II and its aftermath—and partly because of them—my life is a miracle. My family and friends are my greatest blessing. Israel and Judaism will always be the center of my communal life."

I concluded my remarks by reciting a Shaul Tchernichovsky poem:

You may laugh at all my dreams,
But what I dream shall yet come true!
You may laugh at my belief in men,
You may laugh at my belief in you.
But freedom still my soul demands,
Unbartered for a calf of gold.
For still I do believe in man,
I believe in his spirit, strong and bold
And in the future, I still believe
Though it be distant, come it will
That nations will each other bless,
And peace at last the earth shall fill.

The Hebrew term *tikkun olam* means "to repair the world." This remains as paramount today as it was during the nightmare of the Holocaust.

As the matriarch of an extensive family, I know that family unity and togetherness has meant everything to me, and I still continue to strive for it.

My love for Israel and the importance of the survival of our nation has always been a central point in my life and has brought additional meaning to my life. And I hope to see the day that there will be true and lasting peace in that region of the world.

Miracles can happen. I should know.

Epilogue

I would say her greatest quality is her incredible resilience and determination to survive. She has an incredible drive to be alive and a resilience to do whatever it takes to survive. My mother has taught me to never give up. She's taught me to have hope, to have faith, and to fight. It's that drive to succeed. From her example, I've learned that things will work out if you do the right thing.

—Harold Krasner

To me, her best qualities are her strength and her will. Mom taught me about family, the closeness of family, and the importance of keeping the family together. She has taught me about Zionism and the love of Judaism. It was her influence that resulted in all her grandchildren going to Jewish day schools.

She is the matriarch of our family—the one who is always trying to bring everyone together. She always says, "We need to stay together, we need to be together."

—Shirley Krasner First

I've learned perseverance from her. Her perseverance is second to none. She is tough. She's done so much and achieved so much in spite of her being hammered in her lifetime. Wherever she goes, people recognize there is something about her that is potent. What impresses me the most is the effect she has on people and all that she has accomplished.

People often stop me and say, "You're Fanny's son? Wow, she is phenomenal!" I couldn't agree more.

—Milton Krasner

I have four grandchildren under six years old and they are all going to be Orthodox Jews. In large part, that comes from Fanny.

Fanny has a unique ability to make whomever she's with feel like they are her best friend. She loves them so dearly. Every one of her kids thinks they are her favorite, every one of her grandkids and great-grandchildren thinks that as well. And all her friends think they are her best friend. And she treats them like they are.

—Marc Lebovits

(left to right): Milton, Shirley, Marc, Fanny and Harold

FAMILY TREE
1859-2018

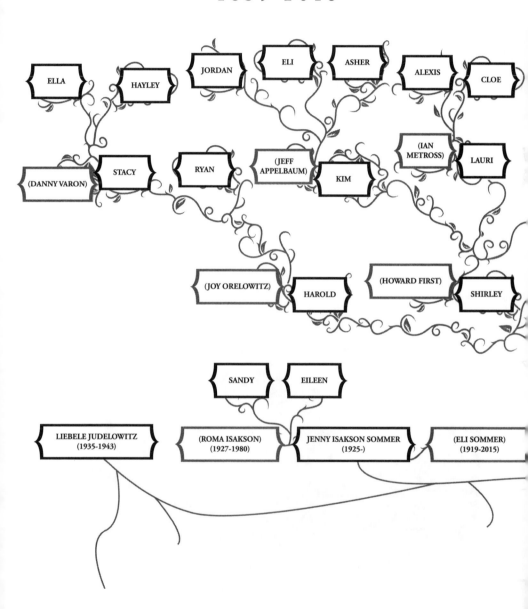

ELLA

HAYLEY

JORDAN

ELI

ASHER

ALEXIS

CLOE

(IAN METROSS)

LAURI

(DANNY VARON)

STACY

RYAN

(JEFF APPELBAUM)

KIM

(JOY ORELOWITZ)

HAROLD

(HOWARD FIRST)

SHIRLEY

SANDY

EILEEN

LIEBELE JUDELOWITZ
(1935-1943)

(ROMA ISAKSON)
(1927-1980)

JENNY ISAKSON SOMMER
(1925-)

(ELI SOMMER)
(1919-2015)

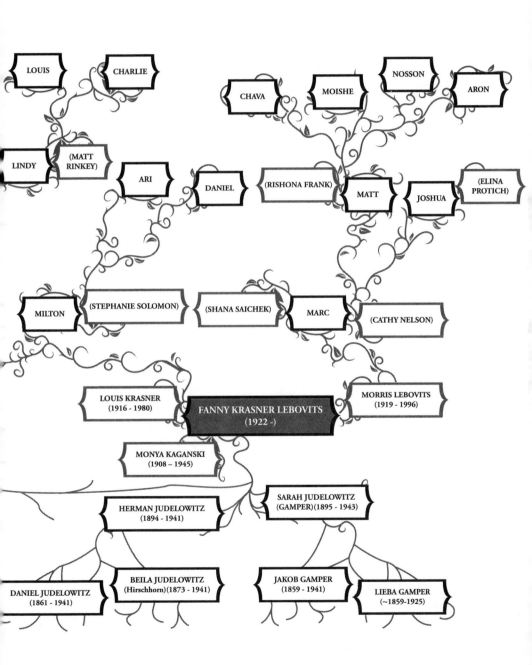

Ultimate Triumph over
Adversity - Family

Glossary

Aizsargi: A paramilitary organization or a militia in Latvia.

Aktion: An operation involving the mass assembly, deportation, and murder of Jews by the Nazis during the Holocaust.

aliyah: Immigration to Palestine.

Aliyah Bet: The clandestine immigration of Jews to Palestine between 1920 and 1948.

anti-Semitic: Feeling or showing hostility toward or discrimination against Jews.

appell: Roll call.

Badanstalt: Spa.

bat mitzvah: A religious ceremony in which a Jewish girl at the age of twelve assumes religious responsibilities.

Betar: A revisionist Zionist youth movement founded in 1923 in Riga, Latvia, by Vladimir (Ze'ev) Jabotinsky.

beit midrash: Study hall.

bris: A circumcision ceremony.

b'riut: The combined health of body, soul, and intellect.

B'tzelem Elohim: Hebrew term that means we are all made in God's image and thus we are required to respect the inherent dignity of every individual no matter their religion, beliefs, race, or affiliations.

chai: The Hebrew word for "life" is a popular symbol and toast and is linked to the number 18.

challah: A braided egg bread.

chutzpah: Yiddish term for "nerve."

daven: To recite Jewish liturgical prayers.

delousing: Process of treating a person or animal to rid them of lice and other parasitic insects.

Eretz Israel: Land of Israel.

Freiheitskämfer: German term for "freedom fighter."

gefilte fish: Ground, deboned white fish.

gemilut chasadim: Yiddish term for "bestowing kindness."

gymnasium: A European secondary school that approximates American high school and the early years of college.

Hadassah: A Jewish women's philanthropic organization; the *largest women's organization* in the United States.

Haggadah: Jewish text that sets the order for the Passover seder.

Hauptwachplatz: The main square in Libau.

Hechalutz: A Jewish youth movement that trained young people for agricultural settlement in Israel.

High Holidays: Consisting of Rosh Hashanah, the Jewish New Year; and Yom Kippur, the Day of Atonement.

Judenfreundlich: Jew-friendly.

Judenrat: The German name for the Jewish Council.

Kapos: German criminals, many facing life sentences, released to supervise the Jewish inmates.

Klal Yisrael: The entire Jewish people.

kinderlach: Yiddish term for "children."

kringle: A pastry in the shape of a pretzel.

madrich: Scout leader.

matzos: Unleavened bread.

Mischling: Term used in Nazi Germany to denote persons deemed to have both "Aryan" and Jewish ancestry.

Passover: A Jewish festival commemorating the liberation of the Israelites from Egyptian slavery.

Pērkoņkrusts: A Latvian ultranationalist anti-Semitic political party founded in 1933.

Nazi: A member of the National Socialist German Workers' Party, which controlled Germany from 1933 to 1945 under Adolf Hitler and advocated totalitarian government, territorial expansion, anti-Semitism, and Aryan supremacy.

raus: German term for "get out."

Reines Judische Fett: German term meaning "pure Jewish fat."

Schutzpolizei: The German uniformed police force.

seder: A ritual feast that marks the beginning of the Jewish holiday of Passover.

Shabbat: The seventh day of the Jewish week and the day of rest and abstention from work in the Jewish tradition.

Shoah: Another term for the Holocaust.

shochet: Kosher animal slaughterer.

shofar: A ram's-horn trumpet used in modern Judaism, especially during Rosh Hashanah and at the end of Yom Kippur.

simchas: Jewish festive occasions.

Simchat Torah: The Jewish holiday when the last verse of the Five Books of Moses is read, the Torah is complete, the chapters ended.

SS: An abbreviation for *Schutzstaffel*, which is German for "protective squadron."

tikkun olam: Hebrew term meaning "to repair the world."

tikvah: Hope.

tzedakah: Hebrew term for "charitable giving."

Unetanah Tokef: A poem that has been a part of the Rosh Hashanah and Yom Kippur liturgy in some traditions of rabbinical Judaism for centuries.

Vaad Ha-Hatzalah: An organization originally established to rescue rabbis and yeshivah students during World War II but expanded to assist all Jews.

Yad Vashem: The Holocaust Memorial in Israel.

Yiddishkeit: The Jewish way of life.

Yom Kippur: The Day of Atonement, the holiest day on the Jewish calendar.

Zachor: Remember them.

zayde: Yiddish term for "grandfather."

zechut: Hebrew word for "privilege or reward."

zhids: Slang Russian term for "dirty Jews."